CONTENTS

FOREWORD   v

INTRODUCTION   vii

1. **CONTROL:** The Good, The Challenging,
   And The Possible   1

2. **FREQUENCY:** The Essential Importance
   Of Timing   12

3. **INTENSITY:** Thresholds And Triggers
   For Results   20

4. **DURATION:** How Long Does It Last?   43

5. **PROBABILITY:** Turn Chance Into Winning   53

6. **CONTEXT:** Interpret And Organize Reality   73

7. **OSCILLATION:** Repetition, Variation,
   And State   92

8. **PRESSURE:** Contact And Force   110

9. **SIGNIFICANCE, RELEVANCE, USEFULNESS**   123

LIFE CONTROL

TAKE CHARGE AND GET AHEAD

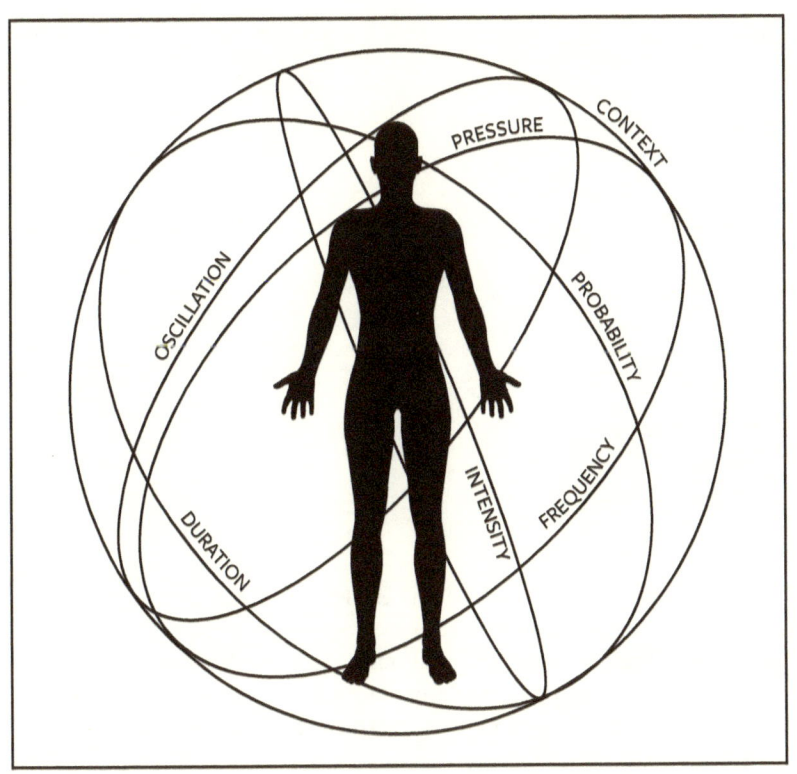

A SMART GUIDE FOR USING SCIENTIFIC
PRINCIPLES TO CONTROL YOURSELF,
MANAGE OTHERS, AND ACHIEVE YOUR GOALS

MARK STEINBERG, PhD

BRIGHT
JOY
PRESS   Bright Joy Press

Paperback: 979-8-9874856-0-6
eBook: 979-8-9874856-1-3

Cover and book design by Mayfly Design

Library of Congress Catalog Number: 2022923344

FOREWORD

Dr. Steinberg's guide to taking charge of one's life is a refreshing and truly accessible contemporary take on scientifically based wisdom. What sets this offering apart is its very successful combination of practical strategies and modern scientific knowledge in neuroscience and behavioral science.

Dr. Steinberg deftly interlaces truisms about consciousness and subconsciousness with brain and behavior functions (and the world that surrounds) through multiple recognizable parameters and down-to-earth examples. These are always amenable to observation and control. According to Steinberg (and to those who came before), they are: *frequency; intensity; duration; probability; context; oscillation;* and *pressure*. Readers will find fascination and truth in how these qualifiers relate to natural phenomena and their own challenges. Dr. Steinberg's unique gift is his ability to make the reader aware of these patterns and their paramount importance in day-to-day life, creativity, and success.

Life Control: Take Charge and Get Ahead will appeal to readers of all backgrounds. You won't need a doctoral degree or a particular theoretical orientation to benefit from the banquet of self-understanding offered here; all you need is the willingness to dive in and grow.

— Cédric Allen, MD

INTRODUCTION

What do people *really* want?

For decades, I've asked this question in many ways, using different language in different situations. In my professional role as a veteran clinical and neuropsychologist, I ask, "What do you really want?" as a natural part of interviewing and establishing a working alliance with patients.

In a broader context, the question may be posed in business (marketing, product development, mediation, or arbitration), legal proceedings, international affairs, personal goals, and the many arenas of human relations and personal ambition.

I've asked myself repeatedly the same question as I've grown through many periods in my own development and life experiences.

What do I really want?

It may be a familiar refrain of your own self-inquiry and explorations in your world.

I will share with you a distillation of the answers to this question—a summary that underpins the reason for writing this book and the value it may provide others toward achieving and obtaining their own answers.

BASICS OF WHAT PEOPLE WANT

Living in America in the twenty-first century brings us all in contact with a cross-section of cultures. Though groups and individuals vary in their desires and aspirations, I witness a commonality of core *wants* that transcends cultural differences and typifies people in "bottom line" striving, goals, hopes, and motivations.

In a nutshell, I found that people want:

1. material comfort, security, and protection;
2. health and control over one's own body;
3. satisfying interpersonal relations (including support and validation);
4. a stake in productive contribution to one's surrounding community;
5. opportunity and ability to "get ahead" in achieving personal goals and a higher standard of living;
6. purpose beyond one's own needs: providing for others—materially, emotionally, and spiritually;
7. living a "worthy" life, according to moral principles and character;
8. power, in the sense of controlling one's own destiny;
9. making a difference in the lives of others and in history; and
10. contentment and peace.

Any hierarchy of needs and wants may be re-prioritized when basic survival needs are threatened or continually deprived. Hunger, loss of shelter, or threat to one's safety become emergencies or crises whose immediacy takes precedence over "higher-order" wants. The precedence of survival's basic requirements remains overriding. When these are reliably provided, we have more leeway and leisure for the consideration of attaining other desires.

It may also be reasonably argued that people's wants are shaped and filtered by economic and opportunities, influenced by political and social climates, as well as prevailing cultural mores and values. While millions struggle to pay bills and afford basic life necessities, others strive for "luxury" indulgences—which seem to them as dire a need as the basics are to others. There is irony in this wide disparity; yet, each of us is dedicated to and motivated by personal needs, circumstances, and ideas about what would make life better.

Balancing one's own desires, ambitions, and even greed can give rise to an ambivalent carousel of feelings, attitudes, and justifications. Relative needs, desires, and cultural influences notwithstanding, it's human nature to want to "get to the next level."

A successful businessperson once told me, "Most people are broke, just at different levels."

My life experience has confirmed that observation, along with my own discovery that most people are also *broken* in different ways at different levels.

Being broke and/or broken is a good baseline for validating our hurts and desires and putting in place a realistic plan to gain better control over ourselves and our lives. This is the essence of what most people want.

INEQUALITIES GIVE WAY TO COMMONALITIES

The "relatively free and liberated" America still has an abundance of racism, sexism, inequality, and oppression. In addition to socioeconomic, political, and class stratification, there remains the stark reality of genetics. Some people just have more than their share of burdens. The sobering message, "I complained about the holes in my shoes until I met a man who had no feet," reminds us to be humble and grateful!

In my view—after many discussions and considerations of inequities, injustices, differences, and analyses of individual and cultural variables—it boils down to this: *People want to be in control of themselves, their power and effectiveness in the world, and their ability to get ahead in their business and personal lives.*

For some, it may be losing weight, prevailing in a competition, or conquering anxiety. For others, getting a degree, a coveted job, or a promotion may be paramount. The particulars vary of course, but the commonality is that we all want more—success, achievement, money, autonomy—control over ourselves and what happens to us as we move along in life.

THIS BOOK IS ABOUT LIFE CONTROL

I call these core common desires *Life Control*. This book is about taking better control of what happens within you and around you—from your health, well-being, and personal habits to your success in forging ahead, making progress, and climbing the ladders that represent for you the ascent to a good, better, and worthy life.

Toward that end, I have analyzed and herein explain and describe in detail seven principles you need to gain better control over your life. These principles are not just abstract concepts (although you will need to use your best smarts to fully appreciate them). They are scientific and practical truths about how the world and people operate.

As you review and study these principals—aided by the many down-to-earth examples and recognizable scenarios provided—you will become more effective and productive in your life. Additionally, as you better understand and implement these principles, you'll gain increasing satisfaction with who you are, as well as what you can accomplish.

These seven principles are not ideas that I invented. Rather, they are distillations and practical, example-filled guides to comprehending and gaining mastery over rules that govern how you and the world really work.

CHAPTER 1

CONTROL

The Good, The Challenging, & The Possible

As we go through life, we find many appealing commodities and goals to strive for and attain. We have wants and needs, feelings and ideas, memories and instincts, as well as countless learned behaviors that influence our desires and ambitions. We live in a world with millions of other humans with whom we share more similarities than differences, despite the occurrence of conflicts and misleading appearances that may make us feel "different," discouraged, or not good enough.

You may be troubled by a lack of focus, direction, or difficulty figuring out and implementing what it takes to get ahead. Perhaps bad habits hamper you, or you struggle with becoming more successful in areas that are important to you and that are valued by our society: finding a place or making a name for yourself, establishing financial security, developing rewarding relationships or skill sets, overcoming flaws, and making progress toward improving your position in life.

Perhaps you compare yourself to others unfavorably, lack sufficient self-confidence, or feel that no matter what you do, you cannot satisfy yourself or others. Possibly your goals seem distant or lack clarity, and/ or you've strayed from the path you once had in mind for yourself. You may be battling emotional impediments, addictions, or self-sabotaging behaviors in the struggle to maintain a steady course toward attaining the goals and outcomes on which you set your sights. You might be haunted by a lack of fulfillment, undermined by an excessive reliance on the opinions of others, and fearful of the potential roadblocks you may see looming before you.

At many turns, life can be daunting, perplexing, and overwhelming, even for those who seem well endowed with advantages and resources to cope and prevail. For those who have floundered for a while, the prospect of taking charge may seem frustrating or out of reach.

Conversely, you may be a person who is already successful. If so, you may be accustomed to having things flow for you. Thus you're probably interested in achieving better or expanded results, improving your efficiency and influence, and possibly reducing your stress and the negative effects of obstacles and undesirable situations and people.

In any case, learning about and practicing several highly effective, scientifically based principles can exponentially enhance the likelihood of your attaining more rewarding desired outcomes. It's all a matter of control.

CONTROL—THE MISSING PIECE

Central to the similarities among people is the need and desire for control. The capacity to handle what goes on around you and within us is fundamental to existence. It enables us to survive and function, as well as to interpret and organize ourselves and the world around us. Control is vital for managing yourself and for determining the outcomes that you want. To be in control is to manage issues, events, actions, and plans efficiently and successfully as you progress toward your desired results.

The difference between success and failure, progress or stagnation, influence or ineffectiveness, often boils down to the issue of being in control. There are, of course, limits to what any of us as individuals can influence, but exercising control over oneself and one's environment can be improved with measurable results by just about anyone who takes stock of and practices the management principles that are available to us in the natural world. Control is not a static entity. Control is dynamic and constantly changing in response to a flow of conditions. Rather than thinking of control as exerting mastery or establishing authority, it is more realistic to consider it as the vibrant interaction with natural forces and the flexibility to reestablish balance and functionality in accord with varying conditions—such as the shifting of expectations as life experiences change us and our values and priorities.

This book teaches how to implement and integrate these positive control principles—how to recognize them, reorganize them in your daily activities, and make them *work for you* to get ahead in the areas of your life that are personally stimulating and materially vital.

It doesn't matter where you are in life—already functional and successful, or down-and-out and underachieving—appropriating these principles will improve your health, your outlook, and your circumstances. This is not a panacea, but rather an invitation to study and implement the natural forces that can help you attain your goals. I am not selling new ideas or gadgets, nor do I have a patent on new products, methods, or realities. I simply put together a down-to-earth, practical package of explanations and exercises to help you harness the control mechanisms that God created in our natural world.

Where this book differs from the many approaches to self-improvement and developing successful habits is in the following:

1. You will be easily able to understand the principles involved in taking charge of yourself and your circumstances—that is, how natural forces are affecting you and how to harness them to help you attain your goals.

2. You will be able to apply these principles in practical ways to form and solidify productive habits and relinquish counterproductive habits (as compared with simply becoming aware of what good habits you need).

3. You will learn how to apply the "take charge and get ahead" principles to specific behaviors and goals of your own choosing and how to measure and reinforce your progress.

4. You will use the "hidden secrets" in these principles to counteract any weaknesses and self-sabotaging tendencies.

5. You will gain the power of harnessing nature's tools that govern and predict behavior.

6. You will become the agent of your own advancement as you substitute productive accomplishment for excuses, stagnation, and other maladaptive behaviors.

Whatever your circumstance, history, and attitudes, please reflect upon this: natural forces, such as gravity, fire, and friction, govern how you maneuver and what results from your interactions. The forces of nature follow rules that are largely predictable (though not always controlled to one's advantage). Similarly, we can use to our advantage the effects of natural forces and their cause-and-effect relationships with our brain-behavior connections to predict and control advantageous outcomes in everyday life.

This is what *life control* is all about.

LIFE CONTROL

Being in control of our life does not imply that we are or need to be a "master of the universe." No one can predict or control all events. Each of us can direct our destiny only to a certain degree. The truth that God is in control provides peace and reassurance, but that reality does not let us off the hook from doing the work of managing ourselves and the ways we progress through this material world.

Life control involves taking charge of the dynamics and principles that underpin and determine outcomes in our internal functioning, our outward behavior, and ultimately in our successes and influences upon the environment and other people.

You don't have to be a "control freak" or micromanage all the details that can easily overwhelm. Successful and highly functional people have habits of attending to the *relevant* and *important* matters without overreacting or constantly responding to urgent crises that can obstruct effective management as well as health and happiness.

People who function soundly, achieve regularly, get necessary things done, and maintain a balanced approach to life's demands, temptations, and rewards have developed a working mastery of what it takes to manage well on a consistent basis. They may not be conversant with the scientific basis of the principles they practice, but they intuitively implement them on a pragmatic and routine basis. Successful, productive people engage life with common sense and experiential know-how. They implement the "do's and don'ts" of taking charge and making necessary and good things happen.

SUCCEEDING AND GETTING AHEAD

We may assume that almost everyone wants to succeed—that is, "get ahead." What does it mean to *get ahead*? Generally, this means *improving upon one's own status and position relative both to oneself* (with respect to previous functioning, performance, and standing) *and in comparison with others*.

Measurable and specific goals are vital in order to monitor and evaluate progress and achievement. But a stark truth is that much of life is relative, as we act in a constantly changing environment with so many variables that affect our comparative position. As a concrete example, our driving speed is easily measured with reference to stationary objects. In contrast, it's very difficult to determine our moving speed by only referencing the images of opposing traffic or of cars going slower or faster than us while moving in the same direction. This example may seem obvious, because you experience this acutely when you drive on the road and pay attention to this phenomenon.

Measuring growth, change, and relativity over time and varying circumstances becomes much more difficult when our attention swerves by emotional impact, environmental changes, evolving values and conditions, and shifting reference points for evaluating change.

Certain aspects of mathematics—particularly quantitative measurement and probability—are very helpful in establishing useful reference points; and you don't have to be a math whiz to use and benefit from these tools. Here's an easy example:

When I look at my elementary school class pictures from first through sixth grades, it is easy to recognize myself (though I looked very different then). I find myself in each of these group pictures, sitting in the front row. This is because I was shorter than most of my classmates *in every grade*. Clearly, I grew in height between first and sixth grades; but relative to my classmates—who were also growing—I remained among the shortest. Thus, it is hard to tell *how much I grew over time* by merely looking at the class pictures, because of the *context*. Indeed, by comparison with my classmates, it appears I may not have grown much at all!

The relevant realities in this example are twofold:

1. My height must be measured relative to myself across time.
2. In comparison with my peers, I will tend to be shorter than most, irrespective of my own significant rate of growth and absolute growth. (This is known as norm-referencing in statistics.)

Both observations are true and relevant. Which aspect I focus upon depends on what I want to compare and for what purpose.

If we are trying to "get ahead" in life, we need to maintain adequate and reliable perspectives on both *fixed* and *variable* reference points. You will learn how to do so systematically by reading about and becoming facile with applying the principles explained in this book.

Whether you are trying to lose weight, drink less, make more money, get a promotion, regain your health, sleep better, or a myriad of other objectives you may have, these are the commonalities of purpose and methods to advance and to document your progress:

1. You need to habitually and systematically monitor and record your "before and after" positions along the way to your goal.

2. You must become familiar with the phenomenon of changing standards as you take steps forward or backward. You may want to adjust your goals and actions accordingly with regard to your rate and degree of progress.

PRINCIPLES FOR TAKING CHARGE AND GETTING AHEAD

The principles this book reveals will help you improve, exert more control over yourself and outcomes involving others, and make decisive strides in targeting and vectoring in on your defined goals. You will find it easier to stay interested and attuned if you anchor these principles to categories and domains that encompass your personal goals. For some examples, see below.

Here are the seven principles needed to take charge and get ahead:

1. **Frequency**
   Frequency is a measure of *how often* something happens.

2. **Intensity**
   Intensity refers to the *degree or strength of a stimulus*, a measure of *how much* of something perceived or experienced.

3. **Duration**
   Duration refers to *how long* something *lasts*.

4. **Probability**
   Probability indicates the *likelihood* of something *occurring or reoccurring*.

5. **Context**
   Context is the background, surrounding structure, conditions, or perspective in which an event occurs and which influences its meaning and interpretation.

6. **Oscillation: Repetition, Variation, and State**
   Oscillation is the rhythmic fluctuation, repetition, and variation that comprises and determines *state*—the particular condition of someone or something at a specific time.

7. **Pressure**
   Pressure refers to the contact and force that exerts influence and effects upon objects, persons, motivation, and outcomes.

These are familiar words we have understood and used in particular situations. Each represents a powerful principle that involves rules applicable to assuming control, implementing and tracking a plan, and following through to achieve desirable results. These principles will facilitate your taking charge of yourself and have a positive influence on the behavior of others and on real world circumstances that will permit you to catapult to higher levels of achievement and success.

STANDARDS, CHALLENGES, AND OBJECTIVES FOR GETTING AHEAD

As previously mentioned, we need criteria by which to measure our progress. There can be many standards and arbiters of change, and you will have your own ideas of what's important for you. These principles will apply to whatever you have in mind.

In general, we may establish common standards by listing categories and domains, which I refer to as *challenges and objectives*.

A list of guidelines for choosing and measuring the range of possible improvements and advancements you might want to make in your life:

Material benefits (wealth, tangible acquisitions)
   Money
   Career advancement
   Desirable possessions

Performance improvement—self

Better productivity
Error reduction
Efficiency—speed, timeliness, cost
Planning and organization
Reliability and follow-through
Persistence

Social relations, interpersonal effectiveness and satisfaction

Influence, persuasion, leadership
People comfort, skills improvement
Tolerance and patience
Compassion, consideration, and sensitivity
Helping and carrying burdens of others

Recognition, acknowledgment, and appreciation

Positive feedback
Popularity
Prestige

Goal attainment and milestones

Achievements—professional and personal
Career advancement
Degrees, licenses, admissions
Personal bests, competitive bests
Accomplishments, awards
Determination, drive, persistence

Health—physical, mental, emotional

Emotional stability
Mental functioning
Recovery from illness
Overcoming addictions
Physical achievements, weight loss
Improved fitness and energy
Better sleep and diet

Response to adversity
> Frustration tolerance
> Weathering setbacks
> Rebounding and persistence
> Emotional control
> Anger management, overreactions

Self-management—neurological
> The internal brain and nervous system self-regulation control mechanisms that influence functioning and affect the challenges and objectives listed

Self-management—environmental
> The outward behavioral manifestations showing control of and influence over the challenges and objectives listed

PRINCIPLES AND PRACTICE

Most people are eager (even impatient) to get on with the practical applications and implementations that will accomplish what they want. Principles, concepts, and theories can be esoteric and even boring. However, they are a roadmap and guide to planning, keeping on course, evaluating, and making adjustments to achieve the desired outcome or destination.

I know we all want to get quickly and practically to the bottom line in obtaining the outcomes important to us—results that are among those listed in the outline previously. To do that effectively—better than we have thus far—we need a deeper and more-comprehensive understanding of the Life Control principles. Then we'll be better equipped to engage and apply them to our advantage.

This book teaches these principles. I've tried to distill important complex concepts into accessible explanations, interspersed with real-life examples. To generalize and apply these principles into transforming results, we need familiarization, recognition, and comprehension. This is my mission with this book. I hope you will acquire deeper understanding of the natural principles that allow you to take charge and get ahead.

PRACTICAL APPLICATIONS

My clinical work and some future writing will be a logical and practical follow-up to implementing the principles delineated in *Life Control*. After explaining the principles that allow and propel a person to achieve greater control, improvement, and success, I will naturally explain how to apply these principles to one's own circumstances. Along the way, I'll enhance the accessibility of these principles through examples and tie-ins to everyday situations.

As you read and assimilate the power of these key principles, keep in mind the specific challenges and objectives to which you may want to apply them.

Bear in mind that understanding the *principles* is important for taking charge and getting ahead before applying them intentionally to manipulate any desired outcomes. To a large extent, we are all already using some of these principles, because they are naturally interwoven with behavior, survival, and practical common sense. My aim is to provide knowledge and a proven plan to make people more effective in this effort.

Please be patient. Book learning can be fun, particularly when there's a payoff in sight. Later in the book, are examples that will connect with your experience. But first, I will provide some needed insight and an overview of what's going on "under the hood" of behavior control.

Enjoy the ride as we delve into the fundamentals of control.

CHAPTER 2

FREQUENCY

The Essential Importance
of Timing

Some may be surprised to learn how the phenomenon of *frequency* influences our perception and shapes our behavior. In common terms, frequency is defined as the rate of recurrence of an event, which is intrinsically linked to the concept of time, and is used as a measurement tool in much the same way the scale is used as a measurement of weight loss or gain when you're on a diet, and the thermometer is used as a measurement of temperature when you are sick.

Another illustration of this basic interrelationship is the fact that Wednesday occurs once every seven days. If you put your mind to it, you could come up with countless other mundane (or esoteric) examples that link the phenomena of frequency and time. If you develop a urinary tract infection and have to go to the bathroom frequently, your urges could be measured in minutes or hours (and might be compared over *time periods* with your rate of going previously). If your relatives visit too frequently, this might be assessed in weeks or months (with the *too* modifier being subjective, of course).

Frequency is a measure of how often something happens. The lapses in time between occurrences are called *intervals*. These intervals can be *fixed* (as in the time between Wednesdays) or *variable* (as in the time between when blue cars drive under a given overpass on a freeway).

Understanding frequency, and recognizing how it influences your habits and choices, play a major role in your taking charge of what happens in your life. Frequency is a key principle in developing control of yourself, the conscious direction of your behaviors, and the responses of others.

In this chapter, I explain the concept of frequency and provide examples of how it operates in everyday life. First it might be helpful to denote the scientific relevance of frequency so you can appreciate how it is interwoven with nature, including the rhythms of our biology and physiological functioning.

FREQUENCY IN SCIENCE

In physical science, we measure frequency by the number of waveforms that occur within one second. So 60 *cycles* per second means that sixty complete sinusoidal curve waveforms occur within a one-second period. The measurement of such cycles assumes they are fixed—that is, a 60-cycle rhythm will have sixty repetitions of the waveform every second.

This definition notwithstanding, frequencies can vary in sequence. In other words, you can have a 60-cycle second followed by several 23-cycle seconds, followed by interspersed cycles of 9-cycle and 14-cycle seconds, and so forth. In fact, these variations are evident in the patterns of nature and our universe. Our solar system has cycles that determine the length of daylight, the different seasons, etc. Within and between those fixed cycles (days, years, winter, summer), we can have varying occurrences of light, heat, rain, etc.

Within our bodies, we have electrical rhythms (brainwaves, or EEG frequencies) that occur in cycles and vary according to biological processes and interactions we have with the world around us. Every person has mixtures of EEG frequencies, and these frequencies (patterns) are associated with types of activities. EEG frequencies in the 1-3 Hz range (one to three cycles per second), for instance, are associated with drowsiness and sleep. EEG frequencies in the 15–18 HZ range are associated with alertness, cognitive processing, and problem solving. EEG frequencies above 40 Hz are usually tied to accelerated motor activity. A broad spectrum of EEG frequencies in our brains correlates with our activities interacting with the world and in managing our internal affairs—the "housekeeping" functions of self-regulation, regeneration and healing, and even the manifestations of genetic attributes over decades of development. Recent evidence suggests that "infra low" EEG frequencies as low as .0001 Hz play a fundamental role in the normalization of central nervous system control (affecting the "fight-or-flight" response) and the degree to which each of us feels secure, safe, and able to trust ourselves and others.

Physiologically and psychologically, feedback loops exist between the "state of body" and the "state of mind." When your brain mechanisms (EEG, neurotransmitters, hemispheric communication activity) are in a certain "state," you will be relaxed or edgy, or perhaps in fight-or-flight mode. Interestingly, these physiological states are highly correlated with and predictive of how you "feel" and also of the types and speeds of thought processes you have while in particular states.

It's fascinating that the continuing progress in neuroscience is confirming and recapitulating much ancient wisdom and practicality regarding the intimate relationships between mind and body, and providing useful tools to enhance our ability to influence and control both body and mind. Brain imaging and EEG neurofeedback (brainwave training) are among the cutting-edge technologies that allow us to witness and modify how our physiology affects our perceptions and motivations and vice-versa. By modifying and better organizing frequencies within our bodies, we can influence and determine how we feel and how we act with surprisingly improved precision, variation, and control.

FREQUENCY AND TIMING

The common usage of the term *frequency* carries implied subjectivity and value orientation. If I like to frequent a certain restaurant, it means I go there a lot. It rains frequently in Seattle, but not as much as in some other places. My mother used to frequently interrupt me. The speaker at the conference cleared his throat with annoying frequency. These are examples of occurrences that may cause a person to take notice and have a subjective reaction.

Our perceptual responses to frequency—that is, taking note when events occur within time constraints that get our attention—are clues that timing really matters in our awareness and responses. But that is only the tip of the iceberg. What underpins frequency are the timing mechanisms that allow us to observe and increasingly take charge of relationships between cause and effect, and steer outcomes in the directions we desire.

Although we might not regularly think in mathematical or scientific terms, we often want to change the frequency of events in our lives. You might want your favorite team to win more *often*; you may wish your boss or your spouse praised you more frequently; you might want to reduce the frequency of (time between) television commercials. Or you might want to have sex more often. Each of these examples reflects the desired manipulation of *timing mechanisms*—specifically, the alteration of frequencies.

Frequency is a function of time. Its measurement can be fixed or variable. The observation and evaluation of frequency patterns can be objective, subjective, or both. The important point is that frequency affects our thoughts, feelings, responses, and behavior patterns. Frequencies are dimensions of the timing mechanisms that determine how the world behaves and how we behave within it.

The phenomenon of frequency is a powerful principle that allows us to observe, modify, and take charge of what happens within and around us.

BECOMING A FREQUENT FLIER

Most are familiar with the term, "frequent flier." Perhaps you even like to accumulate "frequent flier miles" in order to obtain discounts or free goods or services.

Alternatively, a flier is a handbill, leaflet, or notice—a tangible announcement of an event that is about to take place. To make you aware of how frequencies influence us, and to help us become adept in monitoring frequencies and using them to assume control, I use the term "frequent flier" here to mean one who takes material notice of the frequency with which events and behaviors occur. In step with many behavioral scientists, I learned and have practiced the discipline of observing and recording behaviors (in myself and others) for many decades. I constantly observe, monitor, and record frequencies all around me. In my practice of neuropsychology, I record and modify brainwave patterns as infinitesimal as .0001 Hz. Amazingly, this practice helps thousands of people eliminate life-derailing conditions and symptoms, ranging from anxiety to poor sleep to depression, lack of focus, and addictive cravings. The minute frequency difference between .0001 Hz and .0002 Hz can spell the difference between a crushing migraine and complete elimination of symptoms (e.g., headaches, anxiety, depression, sleep problems, and many others).

In more mundane daily life, I observe traffic patterns and times of day (so I can get from place to place with less stress and time expended). I notice when someone is slow to respond and when a person interrupts me or jumps too quickly into a conversation. I monitor my own impatience and the nutritional components of my consumption (how frequently did I eat carbohydrates in the last three days?). I keep track of how many days a week I exercise, and I take my pulse when pushing a workout. I count the number of times per day/week I tell my wife I love her and make gestures of appreciation and sacrifice (yes, that is keeping score of a good kind!).

When testing or evaluating patients, I tally the frequency with which they make certain errors, and I use the data to construct diagnostic impressions and recommendations. If someone is upset or angry with me, I strategically offer empathetic and calming statements and covertly plan and assess the number and timing of such overtures it takes to mollify the emotional negativity. As I teach my dog (or clients) new behaviors, I'm constantly observing and calculating the relationships among encouragements, slight improvements, errors, and the time it takes to develop and multiply the outcomes I want.

Is this manipulative? Sure it is. But it's not malevolent. It is a smart and responsible approach to appreciating and using nature's own rules for taking charge of environmental conditions and imposing order to obtain desired results according to natural rules and consequences.

ARE YOU FREQUENTLY OBSERVANT?

Like me, you also notice frequencies. However, you may not think of them as such, particularly in the "technical" parameters I described. Yet you observe and use frequency information routinely to assist or deter you in making decisions and acting upon them.

You use frequencies in shopping for food. (How often do I eat this item, and when will I run out of something I need?) Frequencies help you decide when to visit the doctor. (The dentist wants me to get a cleaning every six months; if this cough persists, I'd better seek help. Blood in the urine is infrequent, and a single occurrence is a red flag to check it out.) And a pattern of frequent phone numbers on your child's or spouse's cellphone may alert you to suspicious activity.

Consider using frequency data as a scientific aid to becoming more accurate, efficient, and powerful in your exercise of control and leadership over people and events in your life that may, all-too-*frequently* challenge and even dumbfound your capacity to get the results for which you strive.

You can greatly improve the control you exert over circumstances in your life when you become proficient at understanding the impact of frequency on behaviors and use the principles of frequency and timing to schedule and modify the occurrences of events in which you have influence.

Whether it involves losing weight, getting your kids to do homework or chores, or becoming a better athlete, student, artist, or employer, the strategic and skillful use of frequency will increase your production of desired outcomes.

HABITS AS A FUNCTION OF FREQUENCY

We are creatures of habit. The formation of habits occurs through *reinforcement*. This principle of reinforcement denotes the strengthening or encouragement of behaviors contingent upon consequences that raise the likelihood that those behaviors will reoccur. We say that a behavior (noticeable or otherwise) has been reinforced when it *maintains or increases in frequency, intensity, or duration*.

Reinforcement is the behavioral force that controls what we repeat. However, the conditioning process (repeated reinforcement) that shapes behaviors is a two-way street: you can intentionally repeat specific behaviors with the goal of reinforcing them and forming desirable habits—productive behaviors that become automatic.

Habits require *practice*—and practice occurs through repetition, or *increased frequency*.

Many undesirable habits are inadvertently reinforced (thereby strengthened) because they occur frequently and garner attention. Think of the disruptive child who elicits attention by constantly misbehaving. This is a classic example of behavior occurring often enough to sustain a robust and hard-to-break behavior. In this case, heightened frequency becomes a disadvantage.

Conversely, you can use increased frequency to build habits that *work for you*: habits that help you take charge of your own self-management and steer you toward better discipline and achievement. Practicing adaptive behaviors will often also increase your chances of controlling outcomes involving competitive situations and difficult people.

Work, exercise, hobbies, and relationships all require the conscious management of behavioral frequencies to succeed. You must not only practice, but must also manage the *timing* of your practice to improve and maximize effectiveness.

Frequencies are instrumental in the strengthening of habits and in the excitation and inhibition of brain function and control over nervous system response. Our biological rhythms are composed of frequencies. Therefore, we gain advantage by becoming aware of these timing mechanisms and exercising flexibility in shifting among them. A great way to gain access to frequency awareness at an instinctual level is to train your brain using EEG neurofeedback. This training allows your brain to "see" its internal neural activity and make adjustments to be more flexible and functional. During this training, you are actually monitoring and modifying EEG frequencies.

There are, of course, other ways to monitor and adjust frequency in your behavior and in your environment. From praising family members and associates to minimizing indulgence in counterproductive behaviors—there are many conscious and strategic intercessions you can make to take better charge of getting the results you want.

Later in this book, we describe steps for putting this into practice. At this point, we need to recognize frequency as one of the important principles needed and examine how frequency relates to other principles in helping us improve.

FREQUENCY IN COMBINATION WITH OTHER PRINCIPLES

Frequency is a fundamental principle we need to make work for us in order to effectively take charge. It is scientifically and practically interconnected with the other principles I am about to explain. Integrating frequency with the other principles will contribute to and influence outcomes.

How often something happens is one significant factor in determining a result. Along with frequency, other prominent variables factor into the effects that we observe. One such important influence is the principle of *intensity*.

CHAPTER 3

INTENSITY

Thresholds and Triggers
for Results

When we stop to notice, it's surprising how many of our likes, dislikes, motivations, sensitivities, and tolerances are determined by thresholds of *intensity*. How loud we prefer music, how deep or light we like the massage or caress, how we desire our clothing to fit, and what styles appeal to us are but a few examples of the way that intensity influences how we respond to phenomena.

Intensity refers to the *degree or strength of a stimulus*, a measure of *how much* of something we perceive or experience. Our nervous system registers intensity in degrees of excitation, and our brain translates the information into assigned values for tolerance and appreciation.

Thus, our experience of how things taste, whether it's too hot or cold or windy, whether someone is pleasant or annoying, and when we really, really have to go to the bathroom are all reflections of how we feel about and respond to the intensity of particular stimuli.

Of course, intensity varies from individual to individual and from time to time. Nature did not design it to be static, so this flexibility allows for differentiation and adaptation, which are keys to survival.

As we mature neurologically and develop a personality and character, we gravitate toward patterns of comfort and familiarity regarding how much or how little of particular things seems "right." We come to terms with our preferences and limits, and this evolution contributes to our beliefs and habits—the nuts and bolts of our overall persona.

We usually experience intensity as a range: at a certain threshold, we become aware of sensations. If the stimulation keeps increasing, eventually it will become overwhelming. The point at which awareness surfaces is known as a "just noticeable difference" (JND), and the level at which it becomes overwhelming is subjectively perceived as "too much."

For example, think of tasting food and immediately sensing that it should have more salt (or other flavoring). Adding a certain amount of salt will easily reach the "just noticeable difference" threshold, and adding more will readily become too much. Similar instances occur for adjusting the volume of music or television so that it is "just right." Have you ever tried to listen to a caller on the phone whose voice was too low, too loud, or who talked too fast? Now you have some idea of how intensity influences our awareness and comfort zone with "just noticeable difference."

Just noticeable differences (JNDs) are subjective perceptual phenomena, and they apply to both pleasurable and aversive perceptions of intensity. They are part of a control mechanism that helps our nervous systems navigate within a tolerable and favorable range of various intensities.

We seek to arrange the world and modulate our efforts to cope and achieve within this range of comfortable intensity. Insufficient intensity makes life insipid and boring. Too much intensity can result in pain, stress, confusion, irritation, and reduced efficiency.

THE INTENSITY SEESAW

A glut of intensity, or an insufficient degree of it, can create different problems. The set of problems associated with inadequate intensity typically correlates with deficient achievement or lowered performance. In this paradigm, efforts are not strong enough to achieve the desired results or goals. Excessive intensity typically correlates with problematic follow-through, avoidance, and negative emotions. When something is too intense, you just want to get away from it and reduce the unpleasant feelings associated with that event or stimulus.

Two examples illustrate this concept—one with a task, and one involving people:

Suppose you have a report to write. The deadline is near, and you feel the pressure mounting. You find yourself avoiding and procrastinating. Naturally, the longer you put off the task, the more uncomfortable you become, the harder the task seems, and more threatening the looming the deadline becomes. As the intensity of discomfort mounts, you become preoccupied with the burden, and your focus becomes distracted by the need to relieve your anxiety.

Alternatively, you may engage in the task of writing the report, but put forth lackluster effort that yields a less-than-stellar written report, one that falls short of your goal or expectation. In this situation, your concentrated efforts are not strong or intense enough to achieve the competency or recognition you desire.

Next imagine you are at a meeting or gathering in which the person holding or seeking your attention is significantly irritating or annoying. You try to curtail the interaction, but the person bothering you continues, seemingly unaware of his manner nor concerned about its effect. With escalating urgency, you feel the need to escape from this person, possibly at the considerable risk of seriously jeopardizing the purposes and goals of the meeting. In this case, your increased intensity to flee will probably work against you unless you can suppress or camouflage your aversive feelings.

Or imagine the same meeting where, this time, the person or people with you are dull or hardly communicative. Your attempts to engage your audience meet with minimal response or enthusiasm. You redouble your efforts, but to little avail. The strength of collaboration is simply missing, so eventually you assess the merits of the situation and decide to move on, abandoning the motivation to reach the outcome and reward you had anticipated.

INTENSITY AS AN ACTION POTENTIAL

Intensity serves as an accelerant to trigger connections among events in all walks of life. Within your body, neurochemical triggers control the transmission of nerve impulses. Each of your billions of nerve cells has a receiving end (dendrites) and a transmitting end attached by a connecting fiber (axon). The infinitesimal space between these cells (synapse) is a gateway for the release (disinhibition) or stoppage (inhibition) of nerve impulses that transmit the information that makes you function.

The intensity level required for nerves to fire and "jump the gap" from one cell to another is known as an *action potential*. You have natural biological mechanisms to raise and lower these action potentials. In addition, medicine uses this principle in the design and prescription of medications. When you take a painkiller, this substance raises the threshold for transmission of pain impulses. Thus the intensity level for the action potential signaling pain is raised, resulting in the intensity of pain felt being lowered.

For a plane to take off, it must reach a certain ground speed. The necessary threshold represents an intensity threshold, and the transformation occurs between traveling rapidly on the ground and becoming airborne. Similarly, in order to stop your car by braking, a threshold of sufficient friction is necessary.

To dunk a basketball, to jump across a ravine, to reach orgasm, all require specific levels of intensity. In these instances, getting closer doesn't suffice. Whereas much of learning and accomplishment occurs in small steps (known in behavioral psychology as *successive approximations*), in many instances in life, the level of intensity exerted and reached determines the difference between success and failure.

MAKING INTENSITY YOUR ALLY

There are metaphors to describe the stepping up of effort to reach the intensity critical to achieving the desired result. "Digging deep," "giving 110 percent," and "reaching second and third wind" are among such descriptions.

However, the reality is that sustained success depends far more on fine-tuning intensity consistently than on the occasional "superhuman" efforts reported in legends. You can make intensity your ally by learning to identify the intensity levels necessary for JND (just noticeable difference) action potentials in your particular activities and challenges, and then adjusting your habits and pacing yourself to perform steadily, working toward that extra kick that will boost you across the threshold of your desired result. It is much like a runner pacing and striding who, through training and practice, integrates his ability with information about the terrain, competition, and conditions to sprint ahead of the pack and cross the finish line.

In order to make intensity your ally, you must practice your efforts and get realistic feedback on:

1. The amount of effort you need to exert and the quality of that effort (*strength and focus*).
2. The amount and quality of effort required for the desired outcome (*criterion standards and requirements*).
3. The resources and conditions needed to bridge whatever gaps exist between your intensity and the intensity needed to cross the threshold of the desired outcome.

ACADEMIC INTENSITY

To illustrate, take the example of Bob, a smart college student who wanted to get A's. Bob knew that he was bright, and he was very convincing in expressing his desire and motivation to achieve top grades.

But Bob repeatedly earned B's in most of his courses, despite his earnest commitment and many hours of studying. He had reached a point of impasse when he came to me in frustration about his dilemma.

Using the principles listed above, I helped Bob analyze his situation and determine where he needed to make adjustments to achieve his goals. We first took stock of Bob's study patterns, an area he dwelled upon and one that he thought he had mastered. Bob studied for tests regularly, usually putting in several hours a day (thus satisfying the *frequency* and *duration* components needed for success). He couldn't understand how his combination of time consistently spent studying, and superior comprehension of the subject matter, could regularly result in test scores that earned him B's instead of A's. After questioning Bob, I made several suggestions that helped him turn the tide.

First I alerted Bob to the idea that although hard work and consistency are keys to success, he seemed overly preoccupied with his efforts and less aware of his professors' criteria for determining grades as he prepared for exams. I suggested that he write down (for each class) what he thought was required for an A grade on every assignment and test—including specifics and what to study, and how much time and emphasis to expend on each topic. Then I directed him to make appointments with each professor to share his list and his study agenda, and to solicit input, suggestions, and redirection from his teachers, *who were the ones determining the criteria and the measuring devices for evaluating students' performance.* These efforts on my part were a wake-up call for Bob. He discovered that his studying modus operandi was flawed. He was spending too much time studying less-important material, and not enough time identifying and focusing on the key information and concepts that his professors wanted students to learn, and that they were likely to ask on multiple-choice and essay tests and exams. He realized he needed to incorporate this key forecasting concept into his academic regimen, and by doing so, he was soon earning A's.

PHYSICAL INTENSITY

Like so many people, I put on weight and became less active as I grew older. It happened gradually and relentlessly, but the results took their inevitable toll and my health, well-being, and appearance (not to mention pride and ego).

Eventually I determined to improve in middle age and decided to embark upon an exercise program and dietary modifications. I considered myself to be reasonably self-disciplined, and I expected steady, if not rapid, results. However, I did not anticipate the effects of time, the aging processes, and the changes in my body that would obstruct my progress and derail my motivation.

When I was younger, I was a very good athlete. What I lacked in talent and physical dimensions, I compensated by doggedness and dedicated training. It was customary for me to play basketball three hours per day, and (in my late twenties) to run six or more miles daily, lift weights, and sprinkle in some racquetball and bike rides.

As I became more "professional," I earned enough money to eat "well," that is, to satisfy my appetites with rich food out of proportion to what my body needed calorically, could tolerate, and/or could expend. Along with this trend (quickly and indulgently habit-forming), the eventual increasing demands of work and family "ate away" at my dedication to physical fitness.

When I began exercising after more than a decade of sedentary living, I was shocked. I could not even come close to the routines I had easily performed years earlier! I was devastated, embarrassed, and de-motivated. Eventually I gathered myself and persisted, following a routine of exercising at least four times per week for an hour or more. I lost a few pounds here and there, only to gain them back and achieve no real difference, even after many years of stomping at the gym. I felt better by exercising, but my weight remained excessive, and I was unable to achieve the muscle mass and body definition that came easily in my teens and twenties.

I had figured out early on that I could not physically, and would not mentally, push myself to the workout levels required (at least mathematically) to get my body in the shape I wanted. So I resorted to my proven strengths: analysis, observation, and calculated short-cuts (i.e., efficiency). I observed that my moderate treadmill stints left me tired and satiated, but not very sweaty. When I lifted weights, I did many repetitions and variations; and when I finished, I felt loose and strong and better—but I did not feel any burn in my muscles, nor did they become more toned (despite the attendant aches and soreness).

As I churned along with these insipid workouts, I had occasion to notice certain events that I found striking. Although I diligently "exercised," I avoided mundane physical labor whenever possible. I hated to lift or move things. Yet on the occasions when I had to do heavy lifting and moving of objects, I noticed a curious result. *I felt much, much better!* Even my back, which I had learned to conserve and protect after debilitating spinal injuries, felt significantly better after the dreaded stresses of heavy lifting. How could this be? My orthopedic surgeon supplied the "scientific" explanation: "It appears that heavy lifting is good for you. Do more of it."

I noticed something else that was paradoxical too. After my first knee surgery in my forties, I gave up running. The combination of excess weight, degenerative arthritis, and joint pain tanked my hobby of twenty years. I lost my exercise mojo and my endorphins. However, I occasionally had to force my recalcitrant body into a short sprint, such as to catch an airplane flight or to retrieve my dogs when they ran off. Right after these brief and uncomfortable "fight-or-flight" episodes, I noticed that, besides being winded and astonished at my terrible condition, I felt surprisingly alert and alive for hours afterward. What could be happening?

After consulting my physician, I planned shorter and more intense workouts. I interspersed my treadmill routine with several intervals of running slowly for one to three minutes. I also varied my weightlifting by inserting occasional repetitions of 150 percent of the weights I usually pressed or pulled. The results were gratifying. I began losing weight and gaining muscle tone. The secret was revealed: I had stepped up intensity, the needed dimension to trigger the threshold yielding desired outcomes. For me, the slight but important change in exercise intensity made enough difference for my body to respond the way I wanted.

BIOCHEMICAL INTENSITY

Years after I stumbled upon the role of intensity in transforming the efficacy of my exercise regime, I discovered and applied this principle to my diet and nutrition. The combined results are that I've lost thirty-five pounds and lowered my blood pressure significantly, all without medication, surgery, or supplements.

As a disclaimer, I must confess that I like to eat and drink as much as anybody. I also have the willpower of a spoiled child. Yet over a period of time, I completely gave up alcohol, lost dozens of pounds, changed my eating habits to previously unfathomable degrees, and now feel healthier and more-regularly satisfied than when I regaled in self-indulgence, fad diets, and occasional bacchanalias.

Does this sound like a tiresome commercial? I can understand how it might appear that way. But I have no product to sell or specific regimen to exhort. Rather, I am extolling the power of intensity—as one of the five principles that can change your life success—in transforming habits, health, appearance, biochemical functioning, desire, and appetites.

This is how it worked for me:

I had played with giving up alcohol for years. Though I didn't have a drinking problem, I did notice that alcohol increased my appetite, slowed down my metabolism, made me sleep longer, and lowered my inhibitions toward eating rich foods. I gave up drinking for several weeks at a time, only to return to the joy of wine and food pairings. Then I discovered the hardest thing about quitting alcohol: lasagna! For me, the idea of eating lasagna without red wine was unthinkable. I could not dissociate the two. So with great misgivings, I stopped eating lasagna. Amazingly, without lasagna, wine was no longer quite as necessary. I began eating more of the foods that seemed okay without wine. And that was the trick for me to change the alcohol habit. The connection between wine and lasagna was the intensity threshold I had to surmount.

FOOD

Food encompasses a vast domain. To the question, "Do you eat to live, or live to eat?," I realize that I indulgently embody the latter. For most of my life, the natural conclusion to finishing one meal was the transition to anticipating and planning the next one. I once tried diet pills (*Yecch! Never again!*), and have tried many supplements and every "weight-loss" diet I encountered. None of them worked for me. Besides not losing weight and keeping it off, I usually felt unbalanced and deprived. (Again, if this sounds like a commercial, I apologize. Bear with me.)

Yet now I've lost thirty-five pounds, feel *good and stable*, and eagerly sustain a diet that many would consider too stringent. I do it by choice and habit, easily and gradually, using the intensity principle to do its work for me.

For example, I noticed that most of my food intake occurred in the latter part of the day, after work, and before bedtime. This is not a good habit. It is biologically stressful and it contributes to weight gain. But it is an easy habit to form and a difficult one to modify. Here I discovered once again how the intensity principle could help me win battles. Once in a while, I found myself too exhausted to eat before sleeping or, on certain occasions (like after a cross-country flight), unable to obtain suitable food. I went to bed uncomfortably hungry, but too tired to do anything about it. To my astonishment, I'd wake up with an empty stomach—having slept extraordinarily well—and feeling many times better than I usually did. To boot, out of habit, I was rarely very hungry in the morning, even though I'd not eaten the night before. From this repeated observation, I began a habit of eating very little (if at all) one night a week. To stave off hunger, I do any of several things: go to bed early with a cup of tea, remove myself from the kitchen and proximity to food, do yoga stretches, do some administrative work until my eyes are closing, eat a small amount of satisfying healthy protein and fat (like unprocessed nuts). Not only do I avoid excess calories with this routine, but I also reset my nervous system, get restful sleep, and reprogram my habits, so that this is familiar and easier the next time.

Obviously, behavioral techniques are involved, and I have practiced them and discovered the foods that work for me. But the key to success in this endeavor is the strategic use of intensity to achieve my means: I put *just enough* of the right nutrition into my system to satiate my blood sugar so that I don't feel hungry or have rebound effect. I push myself into a nonedible activity just long enough to induce somnolence. I avoid gustatory stimulation and environs just until the stimulation of another activity and body state (like fatigue) becomes *stronger* (slightly more intense) than the motivation to fill my belly. For me, it is more the institution of a satisfying plan than the substitution of a desire—more the resolution of a challenge, than the deprivation of an appetite.

More about food: I drink only water and coffee, two beverages I find satisfying to the point where I desire no others. I eat far more fresh and natural food than processed food. I focus on limiting carbohydrates; when I err or overindulge, I simply compensate and start again by eating salads and less carbs. While this diet would be dire and difficult for most people, it is enjoyable, fun, and reasonably easy for me.

Giving up foods I love would be overwhelming were it not for the intensity principle. By *practicing eating* (that's right, eating takes practice, so enjoy!) certain foods until they become satisfying, I use the intensity principle to form new habits and appetites, and shed maladaptive ones along with their associated cravings.

INTENSITY AS A SOCIAL AND BUSINESS TOOL

The preceding sections show how the intensity principle can help academic achievement and some personal habits. What about using this principle to take charge interpersonally to achieve goals in business and commerce? How can the principles of JND and action potentials be applied to dealing with uncooperative family members, closing a business deal, or getting a job or promotion?

Previously I gave an example of too much intensity in the instance of an annoying or irritating person whose manner may cause you to want to escape from his presence. Surely this type of situation is recapitulated in situations where people grate on each other or rub each other the wrong way. It happens in families as well as in more formal business or social interactions.

Among many witticisms, my father had a pithy saying that rings true when it comes to intensity and the fragility of human efforts. He would intone, "People wear out, but money never does."

My father used this saying to extol the virtue of investment. Yet it apples to the thresholds that result in people *wearing out*—too much intensity from annoying, repetitive, or overbearing behaviors by others, and too little intensity in the direction of achieving the thresholds that trigger crossing the finish line to get the job done ahead of the pack, or at least by the deadline.

Too much intensity projected from another person can become overbearing and wear you out—so you need some coping methods to filter, subdue, or modify the effects of too much interpersonal intensity. Conversely, too little intensity in the area of targeted motivation to finish a task can undermine the efforts to accomplish goals that get things done. Insufficient intensity applied toward reinforcing encouragement, validation, or praise for someone else can weaken how good others feel in your presence.

Earlier in this chapter, I described how the intensity of discomfort that accompanies procrastination can derail productive efforts and, conversely, how efforts that yield little payoff lack sufficient intensity to overcome thresholds needed to launch and complete successful endeavors. Let's examine how these principles can assist with people problems (where emotion and attachments can entangle and muddy situations) and in organizations (where conflicting needs and goals can obstruct group productivity and individual achievement).

DRAMA AND TRAUMA IN RELATIONSHIPS

The story repeats itself like snippets or scenes from a movie played over and over again. You get in the same arguments about money, chores, homework, relatives, computer time, and the list goes on. In brief retrospect, you can recall that the conflict escalated like a fire igniting, but you barely saw it coming before it burst into angry flames. You try to trace back what statement, question, or logic led to this conflagration, and you are bewildered. What did you say or do that caused or deserved such an overreaction? You only know that you are miffed, and that this has happened before and, you dread, it's likely to happen again.

You're caught in the trap of reacting to provocation by the other person, defending your position, venting your feelings, and reiterating your logic. The drama and energy drain may yield despair and the defeating realization that this deplorable cycle is destined to recur, and it eats away at your forbearance and strength.

Your child reacts when you beat the drum about getting homework done before indulging in incessant computer, phone, or screen time. Your spouse complains about one or more of the recurring points of contention in marital dynamics: money, sex, time. These scripts seem to be embedded in the fabric of your life. You are all too familiar with the weariness, irritation, and frustration they engender.

It seems all *too intense*, convoluted, and overwhelming. You feel like the lone voice of reason, and you lament the fact that you are besieged by selfish, obsessed people who won't exert enough motivation and effort—*sufficient intensity*—in the direction you want in order to live peaceably and get important things done.

Ahh—let's apply the intensity principle to take control and turn things around.

First, you must break the cycle of escalation, defensiveness, and aggression by calming yourself. This process also involves detaching somewhat from your emotional investments in desired outcomes. In other words, *you must lower the intensity of your negative emotions*. This takes work, knowledge, and practice. Many techniques can be used to develop this ability. I consider TFT and neurofeedback among the best options. (See my book, *Living Intact: Challenge and Choice in Tough Times* for a comprehensive review and detailed explanations of these techniques.)

Second, you must outline in clear, simple terms the three factors that will get the job done and satisfy both parties in the drama. Here are some role-playing examples of communications that employ the above concept:

1. The amount and quality of effort (*strength and focus*) currently exhibited.

   ✓ "You've spent an hour in front of your books after two hours of avoiding and making excuses. But you've only focused on your homework for twelve minutes."

   ✓ "You've hardly spent any time with me—just you and me, apart from family routines and responsibilities—over the past week, twenty minutes at most."

   ✓ "To my knowledge, you haven't made a budget to pay down our debt, nor have you allocated any funds for that purpose in the last two months."

2. The amount and quality of effort required for the desired outcome (*criterion standards and requirements*).

   ✓ "You need to spend at least one hour of concentrated time-on-task on your homework before I review it and assist you."

   ✓ "Spending fifteen minutes relating together, just you and me, at least five days a week will make me feel satisfied and connected to you."

   ✓ "Two hundred dollars per month toward this higher-interest credit card debt will reduce X percentage of the debt within a year. Also, the first month you pay it will go a long way toward making me feel more secure and that we are a team."

3. The resources and conditions needed to bridge whatever gaps exist between your intensity and the intensity needed to cross the threshold of the desired outcome.

   ✓ "After every five uninterrupted minutes you attend to your homework (no talking with anyone else about anything), I will drop a coupon into the piggy bank. After you earn twelve coupons, you can trade them to me for assistance with your homework questions and for one hour of TV or computer time."

✓ "We need to plan and set aside time each day in advance, or it won't happen. *You* have to write this down on your calendar, and show it to me before you leave in the morning."

✓ "By eliminating three restaurant dinners and six takeout dinners a month and not going to that entertainment event, we'll save enough money to pay the monthly commitment to reducing our debt."

By using the intensity principle to break the cycle of emotional overreaction and entanglement, and by tying it to successive approximations with *specific* JNDs and action potentials (e.g., twelve coupons earns an hour of TV; fifteen minutes a day reestablishes a satisfying connection; eliminating this number of these expenditures each month will make form successful teamwork in reducing or debt), you can take charge of debilitating and unproductive interactions and habits in your family relationships.

INTENSITY IN COMMERCE AND ORGANIZATIONS

To illustrate how the intensity principle can help in business, let's consider two different situations—one in which more intensity is needed to get the job done, and another that calls for a reduction in intensity to result in a better outcome.

Most of us endure many demands upon our performance and expectations of continued productivity. For some, it may seem that no matter what gets done, more is required. The constant demand is poignantly summed in the saying, "What have you done for me lately?"

MORE INTENSITY

This tension is acutely relevant in the domain of sales and marketing. There is always a press for new business as well as the attendant responsibilities in caring for and satisfying existing clients and customers. In addition to the careful allocation of time, "go-getters" must make a habit of *intensifying* or ramping up calls and engagements with existing and potential customers. Experienced salespeople know that success requires working through the "numbers." Of course you must have a worthy product, skillful techniques, and pleasing social skills— but the bottom line will depend upon how many leads are generated and followed with persistence and thoroughness.

This routine is challenging, even for crackerjack producers. Initiating contacts requires a replenishing supply of motivation and energy. Obviously, the rejection factor plays a huge role in deterring motivation and chipping away at persistence and confidence. Even competent and experienced people build up anxieties and avoidance tendencies from the relentless flow of disinterest and rejection. This is the bane of those involved in sales.

In these situations, more (or sustained) intensity makes the difference between success and advancement or failure and stagnation. If you are engaged in such an enterprise, you *know* this; the challenge is how to escalate and keep the intensity going.

Here are some keys to employing this principle:

1. **Make a plan.**
   Outline a proposed and realistic number of calls/contacts you think will move you to the level of performance you want. Remember that at the outset, you are launching an estimate, one you will continually revise according to your practical experience and results. Write down the plan for reference and reminders. Most people are far from accurate in their assessments of what they can get done, how long it will take, and how much is involved.

People low-ball or overestimate their intended performances. These miscalculations break down confidence and discourage motivation. They are natural detractors from persistence and intensity. However, you need these estimates as beginning and reference points for formative revisions. It is natural and helpful to adjust the parameters of intensity. Just think of your habits of exercising, eating, or listening to music—sometimes more, sometimes less, sometimes louder or softer . . .

2. **Activate your plan and keep records.**
   You need data to evaluate your performance and progress. These records need not be meticulous or time-consuming, but they should be consistent and accessible. Write down indications of your activities, including the results and follow-ups. There are many easy-to-use tools that make such tasks quick and easily retrievable. Here is an example of a brief tracking system I use on one of my databases to review communications, interactions, and to prep me for next steps:

Message	7/5/2016	7/16/2016	
Spoke	7/9/2016		
Emailed Me			
Emailed Them	6/28/2016		
Question	Do you treat anxiety and sleep problems?		

3. **Reinforce sustainable increments of activity.**
   At the outset, you may have ambitious plans to initiate twenty contacts a day. It may turn out that such a plan was unrealistic or too taxing; perhaps five contacts happens to be doable. It may be enough to propel you to the

next tier of meeting goals. If so, then focus on sustaining the new level of activity. Reward yourself for achieving this plateau—rewards (or good consequences that follow certain behaviors) become *reinforcements* when they *increase the likelihood of the behavior re-occurring*.

4. **Reduce or eliminate your negative emotions and avoidance.** The quickest and most-effective way to dispatch negative emotions and their untoward effects on productive behaviors (including avoidance and procrastination) is to use TFT (thought field therapy). These techniques are discussed and referenced throughout this book. Specific step-by-step instructions on self-administration of TFT methods are outlined in my book, *Living Intact: Challenge and Choice in Tough Times.*

   Sometimes the challenge of ramping up intensity can seem daunting or aversive. These are the times to employ TFT procedures as your great ally.

5. **Continually adjust standards and estimates of what's doable.** Living requires constant adjustments. This comes as no surprise to adults. However, many people continue to have difficulty with the imperfections in themselves, their plans, and the way the world works. This becomes especially apparent and detracting when it comes to setting achievable goals and objectives. Consider the sayings, "Rome wasn't built in a day," and "Inch by inch, life's a cinch; yard by yard, life is hard."

   When you're trying to ramp up intensity, your initial ambitions and estimates will likely have to be tempered by what you find is doable along the way. Most often, the reach exceeds the grasp, and targets have to be brought closer and toned down. Sometimes though, we need to stretch and become bolder. The mind and body grow through being challenged, as long as the challenges are not so overwhelming as to squelch observable progress and enthusiasm.

As you ascertain what levels of intensity are rewarding and sustainable for your particular efforts, you learn to make the adjustments that carry you forward and give the "biggest bang for the buck" on your intensity investment.

6. **Reinforce your consistency.**

The important step after reinforcing incremental intensity is to reinforce *consistently increased intensity*. For example, if you manage to make five contacts on a given day, see if you can establish a pattern of five contacts on three days per week for three weeks. When you encourage, reinforce, and habituate to the "new normal" of increased intensity/activity, you will establish new standards of performance that become more automatic and achievable. This applies to many areas of life, including exercise, academic learning, and others.

Notice that by reinforcing consistency, you are combining the principles of *intensity and frequency* to work harmoniously together and boost the natural effects.

LESS INTENSITY

Working with people can be difficult. Whether you're in an office or institutional workgroup environment or you deal with clients/customers on a repeated basis, the habits and manners of others can become grating over time or simply rub you the wrong way. It may seem that you have to force a smile and try to get along to avoid conflict or reprisal that can be threatening to your job and security.

In most of these situations, it's helpful to reduce the intensity in feelings, perceptions, and potentially troublesome interactions. This applies to both your perception of the intensity of others and to their perception of you. Too much intensity (or perception of such) is tantamount to "coming on too strong" and can be aversive and result in irritation, defensiveness, faultfinding, and avoidance.

So what can you do to lower intensity?

1. **Reduce or eliminate your negative emotions.**
   As discussed above, eliminate your negative emotions and aversive reactions using TFT. As many years as I've been using these techniques on myself as well as helping others, I'm continually amazed by how other people look when I'm calm and unfazed. Getting rid of negative feelings and reactions does not change my opinions of the inappropriate (and sometimes ridiculous and offensive behaviors) of others. It allows me to remain calm, stay engaged where necessary, and use discretion and diplomacy to make tense situations less difficult and more prone to good outcomes.

   Eliminating negative emotions is the most effective and quickest way to reduce aversive intensity and provide insulation against intrusive or annoying people and the reactions they provoke. Though you may be limited in your control of the requirement to interact with certain individuals, your tolerance and self-control can be literally at your fingertips through the strategic self-administration of TFT.

2. **Consider reframing with flexibility and compassion.**
   While *putting yourself in another's shoes* is an old and wise admonition, here's a new twist: make a practice of assuming that your emotional reactions and umbrage to difficult people are laced with overreaction. You can be "right" and have lots of justifications, but nonetheless react (even internally) with ideas and feelings about the other guy that are far from being in touch with his feelings and point of view.

The idea here is not to disown your logic and emotion, rather to filter your aversive responses by focusing on the outcome you want (possibly even making the best of a bad situation) and allow for your "adversary's" limitations and burdens. Exercising compassion is far from excusing someone; it's seasoning accountability with forgiveness and mercy. By doing so, you don't give up what's yours; instead, you expand yourself and your capabilities. Egos are busybodies who love to be involved, even where they don't belong—and conflict is a breeding ground for the hostile infectious takeover by ego. Beware!

If you can make up some reasons to forgive and be sensitive to someone who's harassing you, then you're well on the way to taking covert control of the situation. Being smart, sensitive, and victorious in persuasion and acceptance is indeed preferable to being "right."

3. **Learn, rehearse, and practice nonthreatening communications.**

   I love to disarm hostile or cantankerous people by agreeing with them! This doesn't mean I *really* agree with them or that I renounce my values, opinions, or even my strong feelings. What it means in practice is that I own the message the person is sending and I receive and complete the communication by saying things that defuse the other's anger/frustration and give that person the clear message that I know and accept their feelings (against me).

   For example, I'm apt to say things like, "Joe, I can see you're very upset with me and that I must have done something to cross you. I'm really sorry that I upset you—please take that seriously. I'm not quite sure what I did that's bad, and I want to understand from your point of view. Please be patient with my ignorance and clarify for me *what specifically I did* that was not right."

Here's another example: "Obviously you're right about *feeling* offended (taken advantage of, etc.). Help me to understand what I missed or overlooked. I certainly didn't want to upset you . . . but *I'm having trouble seeing what exactly is unfair* in this situation. Perhaps you could explain it to me by *stating what rule was violated*."

You can devise and practice many such judicious and tactical comments and make them part of your repertoire to defuse antagonism and lessen the intensity that interferes with your inner peace and the attainment of your goals.

4. **Decrease frequency and duration where possible.**
   Let's include an obvious and natural solution for too much intensity: strategically and intentionally limit and lower the frequency and duration of your exposure to the stimuli that are too intense.

   Leaving a noisy nightclub or construction site would not seem avoidant, but rather an appropriate response to an overbearing situation. (Of course, you wouldn't abandon a friend who's depending on you; nor would you drive recklessly to get away quickly from an intrusive, discordant—these would be emotional overreactions.)

   Similarly, when someone or some environmental situation is consistently bothering you, do your best to reduce or limit your exposure. The difference between "freaking out" or running away, and calmly and purposefully removing yourself from too much noxious stimulation, is the difference between being controlled and taking control.

Hopefully you are beginning to see glimmers of how you instinctively respond to situations that require more or less of intensity and how you can take charge of and manipulate the strengths and thresholds of stimuli that affect your productivity and control. Throughout the book, you can find more examples and applications of this principle to different areas of your personal habits and exertions of influence upon your environment.

You've experienced glimpses of how frequency and intensity work in tandem in natural situations, often in concert with the influences of *duration*, our next important principle in helping you take charge.

CHAPTER 4

DURATION

How Long Does It Last?

One of the most important dynamics that weaves throughout the universe is *time*. At many levels, we are usually aware of time and its relevance to our perceptions and activities. Time is so fundamental to physics and the workings of the universe that great thinkers have incorporated its importance into their theories and formulas. Albert Einstein's groundbreaking theory of relativity is based upon time—specifically, that what we perceive as the force of gravity, in fact, arises from the curvature of space and time.

If abstract theories do not compel you, consider Einstein's simpler, practical explanation of relativity: "When you sit with a nice girl for two hours, you think it's only a minute, but when you sit on a hot stove for a minute, you think it's two hours. That's relativity."

DURATION AS A FUNDAMENTAL PARAMETER

How long something lasts is measured in time. The length or extent of that time period is *duration*.

Duration is integral with our actions and perceptions. How long you sleep matters, as do the intervals of heat you apply when cooking.

How long you can hold your breath or continue to swim may affect your swimming prowess, or perhaps might even save your life in deep water.

Time of continuation pervades the quality and outcome of so many things we do and perceive. Musical notations and variations are measured in time signatures. "Hang time" (seconds a player can stay in the air) is a basketball virtue, and duration of exercise is a determinant of training effects and fitness.

Duration interacts with frequency and intensity to determine the specific outcome of an activity or experience. Moreover, duration often controls whether reinforcement of a behavior occurs, thereby influencing the probability of that behavior reoccurring and strengthening. Said simply: duration is a key factor in whether you receive a payoff for efforts put toward a certain goal or outcome.

For instance, if you are studying, exercising, or practicing an instrument, the amount of time you stay on task is fundamental (and usually proportional) to your mastery of the skill and your successful demonstration or performance. Indeed, you must practice often (frequency) and correctly (intensity); but in order to reach the rewards, you must sustain a sufficient duration, or "staying power." When your staying power achieves the duration adequate for accomplishment or mastery, you will have strengthened your performance and the likelihood that you will engage in this behavior again (thereby forming a *habit*).

PERSISTENCE

In a tale about a man who tried to draw water from a well, he cranked the mechanism at the top of the well that held the bucket deep below by a rope. He cranked and cranked for a long while, expecting the bucket of water to appear from beneath the surface, and pausing only to wipe the sweat from his face. After toiling for an extended time, the man became discouraged and abandoned his efforts. What he didn't know was that the bucket of water was just inches beneath the shaft of light illuminating the inside of the well. Had he continued a minute longer, he would have succeeded in getting the well water.

Sometimes we grow weary and give up. Often our persistence is discouraged when we can't see the light at the end of the tunnel (or beneath the top of the well), or because we are unaccustomed to "digging deep" for just a bit longer, while continuing to be motivated by the lure and sense of the payoff.

DURATION AS A THRESHOLD AND TRIGGER

How long something lasts is often related to the efficacy and intensity of the stimulus. The longevity may also trigger reactions that depend upon the stimulus continuing for a certain amount of time.

For example, physical exercise must be carried on long enough to stimulate circulation, release endorphins, and promote strengthening and cardiovascular improvement. In addition to the staying power needed for improved fitness, sustaining vigorous activity usually leads to a "second wind" in which the subjective experience of the exercise is more readily tolerated for a longer period of time, thus making more available the benefits of endurance.

Consider this example of how I used the duration principle to advance my physical training when I was in college: In my early twenties, I was accustomed to playing basketball for hours at a time. Though I could run and jump with high intensity in short bursts, I was unaccustomed (and unfit) to sustained running at a slower pace for long periods of time. I was a sprinter, not an endurance runner. However, I decided I wanted to run distances, as I'd read and heard about the particular benefits of such exercise. I also wanted to compete in road races. I encountered problems in becoming quickly winded when I tried to run a mile or two, even though I was in great basketball shape. This was mostly due to my habit of sprinting instead of pacing myself for the long haul. I had to restructure my training and practice.

I went to the local high school track and practiced running up to a half-mile at a time. It was embarrassing and frustrating to me that I couldn't even run a consecutive mile at first, as I fancied myself an athlete. So I developed a strategy: I ran a quarter-mile and then a half-mile at a time. I rested for ten minutes—then I ran another quarter mile. After about a week, I rested five minutes between the two running episodes. After a few days, I shortened the rest period to two minutes, then one minute. Eventually I was able to run a mile without resting! I exulted in this accomplishment. Soon I ran a mile, rested for fifteen minutes, then ran another mile. Gradually I shortened the rest interval between miles, as I adapted. Within several months, I was running six miles a day.

The increased duration contributed to a new type of fitness and opened the way for me to experience a second and third wind, improved mental resolve and clarity, and a variety of new social and competitive venues. Without knowing it at the time, I was discovering and combining the principles of frequency, intensity, and duration—modulating each to attain my goals.

SEMINAL ROLE OF DURATION

There are many other examples of the seminal role of duration in causing a desired or favorable effect. In massage, for instance, just the right amount of extended pressure on muscle fibers and nerves allows knots to unwind, muscles to relax and lengthen, and nerves to fire (or stop firing) in ways that bring relaxation and a loosening of painful tension and cramping.

In sports, the length of the competition affects the fatigue levels and skills of the competitors—and not just for endurance-oriented events (like marathons), but for team sports where the abilities of players and teams to "rebound" or "step up" in the latter portions of the game factor heavily in tipping the scale toward victory for those who can endure and prevail.

In workplaces, duration is often a prime factor in determining salary and wage increases, as well as in accruing vacation and sick time. Length of service also influences retirement benefits, and it factors into job promotion.

To increase competence or to gain sufficient skill and knowledge to pass exams or perform certain duties, duration of practice is highly correlated with success.

Duration is also crucial in matters of faith, patience, and forbearance. How long you can put up with stress, uncertainty, adversity, and suffering will influence your spiritual outlook, your self-confidence, your steadfastness, reliability, and maturity. (Of course, everyone has limit.)

To "keep on keeping on" reflects how duration plays a pivotal role in adaptation and the grit that is instrumental to successful outcomes.

DURATION AND REINFORCEMENT

Though prolonged duration is often correlated with more successful outcomes, viewing duration as a variable that can be tweaked and adjusted is important. Shorter durations are sometimes more helpful than longer ones. This was the case in helping me string together running stretches into longer workouts and races by shortening the duration between miles as I trained (as in the example above).

Shorter durations are also extremely helpful in shaping step-by-step behaviors from scratch. Keep in mind the truism that "inch by inch, life's a cinch; yard by yard, life is hard." When you are trying to form a habit that's not yet a part of your behavioral repertoire, doing the new behavior for a very short time at the beginning is more likely to lead to repeating the behavior. Whether exercising, studying, playing a musical instrument, or cleaning and organizing, engaging in the behavior for several minutes will help you have a better experience than if you try to do too much and become tired or frustrated. The more successful and satisfied you feel with your performance, the more likely you are to repeat the behavior. That's how habits form. When a consequence follows a behavior that increases the likelihood that the behavior will reoccur, we observe that the behavior has been *reinforced* (strengthened and more likely to happen again).

Strengthening the behaviors you want is all about *payoff*. If you perceive reward (compensation, satisfaction, recognition, even hope), you will be more likely to repeat or revisit that behavior.

Duration is a powerful dynamic in reinforcement. You can use duration strategically to *shape* or step up behaviors you want to increase, both in yourself and others.

USING DURATION TO INCREASE BEHAVIORS INCOMPATIBLE WITH BAD HABITS

Suppose you have a misbehaving child. The typical array of attention-getting, annoying, and disrespectful behaviors the child displays can coerce you into responding with displeasure, corrections, and sanctions. You may feel compelled to criticize, remonstrate, or intervene in squabbles, defiance, or avoidance. As logical and responsible as it seems, such actions are almost always a trap—your responses reinforce the bad behaviors.

You're "damned if you do and damned if you don't." If you respond—even calmly and responsibly—you end up reinforcing the very behaviors you want to eliminate. If you don't respond, the child just carries on with what he wants to do or not do, creating havoc and controlling the outcome. What's a parent to do?

Here's where the strategic use of duration becomes your ally. Let's say your child misbehaves quite often: perhaps he does something out of line every few minutes. You could use duration as a tool to correct the misbehavior by substituting and reinforcing an alternate behavior that's incompatible with the bad behavior.

Try the following:

1. Take a baseline of the time between bad behaviors—in other words, how long your child typically goes before committing a transgression. Let's say he usually goes (or cannot go longer than) fifteen minutes before complaining or getting into mischief. You might then estimate that the probability of his going longer than thirty minutes without misbehaving is close to zero, and the probability of his misbehaving after twelve minutes is about 50

percent. Using these figures (subject to needed adjustment), you might estimate that the probability of his going longer than seven minutes without misbehaving is about 80 percent.

2. Eighty percent success rate is a good parameter for reinforcing behaviors. When people are close to 100 percent successful, they feel good, but new learning and behavior change is not likely to occur. When the success rate drops near 50 percent or below, frustration increases, motivation is reduced, and trying or reengaging drops off. If you intend to encourage and shape a behavior, setting the bar (reinforcement contingency) at 80 percent is a favorable threshold.

3. Since your child (in our example) is 80 percent likely to refrain from misbehaving for seven minutes or less, you could systematically "reward" him for seven minutes of "good" (nontransgressive) behavior by immediately providing a treat or a coupon, point, or token for something he really wants. Since you have tracked his behavior and speculate that he can often go for at least seven minutes without misbehaving, it is likely that he will be repeatedly successful in meeting your criterion and earning the reward. Thus "good" behavior is reinforced (more likely to reoccur).

4. Gradually you can lengthen the time it takes for him to be reinforced: perhaps ten minutes for a day or two, then fifteen minutes, and so forth. By doing so, you are *incrementally shaping* the length of time he is likely to exhibit the good behavior you want. By keeping the increments small and reasonable, monitoring his success rate, and keeping it at about 80 percent, and gradually—almost imperceptibly—increasing the duration necessary for the payoff, you are stretching the periods of good behavior and forming better habits of interaction for you and your child.

This is one good way to use the principle of duration to your advantage.

Another example: Let's say you want to cut down on drinking, smoking, or eating certain foods. Using the same method outlined above, take stock of your patterns by *writing down* (specifying dates and actions) your baseline behaviors. Perhaps you are drinking or eating dessert every day. Thus the probability of indulging daily is 100 percent—or inversely, the probability of abstinence is zero. Then ask yourself—and experiment—what is the length of time for which your probability of abstinence is 80 percent? If you drink or eat sweets at 7:00 p.m., maybe the 80 percent threshold is at 6:00 p.m.. If so, plan two things to happen at 6:00 p.m.:

1. You need a diversion away from drinks and/or sweets. Perhaps plan a larger meal earlier so you'll be less tempted to indulge subsequently; or plan to be around people or in a situation where drinks or desserts are not available.

2. Plan and give yourself some nonedible reward to reinforce the likelihood that you will do it again—go one evening without indulging. Make the reward *substantial*. Remember you are trying to turn the tide on an unwanted habit that has the strength and sway of reinforcement history. In order to be successful, you must use the lure of a strong incentive to overcome the power of previously reinforced habits. Substitution and incompatibility of behaviors are the key concepts to move forward in a positive direction.

When you are able to go one day without indulging, rejoice, congratulate yourself (perhaps even tell a confidant), and *make sure to reward yourself with something other than re-indulgence in the problem substance.*

When you are ready (probably sooner than you might imagine), try stretching abstinence to two days. Remember to reinforce yourself with the payoff!

Eventually, reduced indulgence or abstinence will become a powerful payoff; but in the beginning and interim, use a concrete reward you will anticipate and enjoy—perhaps something you buy for yourself. Don't worry that you're "bribing" yourself or forming a new over-indulgent habit. This is a strategic tool used temporarily to break a bad habit; you're not likely to become" addicted" to the intervening tool. You will become accustomed to the new and more positive habit. When this happens, the need to keep reinforcing it materially will fade.

DURATION AS A CORNERSTONE FOR SUSTAINABILITY

The previous two examples show how the endurance principle can be used to lengthen the time periods between undesirable behaviors. In the first example, "good" behavior can gradually be reinforced and lengthened to change the ratio of cooperative behaviors to uncooperative ones.

The second example shows how to use duration as a deterrent to habitual indulgence: gradually increase the intervals of abstinence until refraining from indulgence becomes the "newer normal" for the brain, the appetites, and ultimately the behavioral frequency and habits.

At the beginning of this chapter, I shared an example of how I used progressive duration to improve my capacity to run longer distances. Thus you see how the duration principle is instrumental in directly augmenting desirable behaviors and indirectly reducing undesirable ones.

As you take control and program yourself to reach goals, you will become more aware of and interested in behaviors that are *sustainable*—that is, behaviors that "run themselves" without much effort on your part to ramp up or consciously intervene. Many different behaviors contribute to competence, confidence, and productivity. Common to most of these is the central component of *time on task*. Sustained focus and perseverance are required for success in most walks of life and at any stage of engagement and eventual mastery.

Whether the task requires mental concentration, physical endurance, or practice time, necessary and worthwhile endeavors reach fruition when adequate periods of duration are mixed with the frequency and intensity needed to master the task or get the job done.

Life is challenging with periods where all one can do may be to hang on and survive. Eventually these rough patches lighten and pass. If you're determined to take charge and get ahead, recognize and practice persisting for longer durations at the behaviors that will propel you toward your goals.

In so doing, you not only achieve tangible progress—you also acquire life wisdom, confidence, security, and an increased capacity to weather adversity. These accrue when you learn and practice the habit to "keep on keeping on."

Generally, increasing duration to sufficient thresholds is an integral part of getting desired results and achieving objectives and goals. However, continuation in a task just for the sake of determination must be guided and tempered by an assessment of progress along a roadmap of expectations and evaluations of the anticipated outcomes. Otherwise you may fall victim to the old trap of "doing the same things (unsatisfactorily), but expecting different results.

The principle discussed in the next chapter serves to balance persistence and effort with an understanding how they influence the odds of success and a guidance system for making adjustments to improve those odds. This is the principle of *probability*.

CHAPTER 5

PROBABILITY

Turn Chance Into Winning

"There are three types of liars: liars, damn liars, and statisticians."

—Mark Twain

Probability refers to the likelihood of a particular event happening. We may hear on the weather report that there is a 40 percent chance of rain; or, that the chances of winning a lottery jackpot are one in a hundred million per ticket. We typically think of probability as a mathematician's formulaic assessment of how likely it is that an event will occur—and that's true. However, we use probability all the time to predict what's likely to happen in everyday life and to assess the risks and benefits of particular courses of action.

As a simple example, you use probability every time you change lanes on a highway. Prior to your move to change lanes, you calculate the risk that another vehicle will be in your way and potentially result in a collision. As a function of experience, this is so automatic and routine that you hardly think of changing lanes as a risk assessment; but it is, even though you don't consciously use a math formula. In unusual or less-familiar traffic or weather conditions, you may pay more attention to your decision-making and adjust your driving accordingly. In making driving decisions, you "win" at such a high percentage of the time (that is, you don't get into accidents), that the probability algorithms you subconsciously and routinely use happen "under the radar" of your conscious planning.

Industries such as banking and insurance would not be profitable if they didn't rely on probability data to make astute business decisions about lending and rates. A past track record is a prominent factor in predicting future outcomes. Athletes and coaches use probability to anticipate their opponents' tactical moves and strategies and to adjust their own performance and defenses.

Good test-takers anticipate what questions and topics exams will cover. Keen business people handle presentations and customer interactions by preparing for likely concerns and objections.

For your commute to work, you incorporate the time of day, day of the week, weather conditions, and other factors to determine how long your travel will take.

Government agencies use probability to assess the threat and risk of terrorism. Doctors, scientists, and researchers use statistics to predict the likelihood of developing a disease, acquiring an infection, or healing from an injury. Dating services and law enforcement utilize probability to profile behavior. Planning committees use probability to predict future growth and community needs.

We all use probability daily in a myriad of ways from guiding ordinary functioning to predicting the most likely outcomes in novel or unfamiliar situations. We combine past experience with current conditions to anticipate how soon we will really need to use a bathroom or how long we can go without eating before becoming fatigued or irritable. We rely on probability to forecast people's reactions to our emotions, overtures, and grievances. We form preferences, biases, and even prejudices based on our accumulated personal data with groups of people and situations bearing similarities to what we've previously experienced.

Given our inherent and integral need to assess risk, predict outcomes, and modify our actions and expectations, it's not surprising that the awareness and facile manipulation of probabilities can play a key role in success in so many areas of life.

STARTING WITH WHAT YOU KNOW

How then can you use probability to increase your successes, keep yourself motivated, avoid or minimize unpleasant outcomes, and help your attain your goals?

You don't need complicated formulas or computer-assisted statistical models. You do need to develop and hone your skills of observation and analysis, drawing upon the accumulation of your experiences. From these experiences, you make *assessments of cause and effect,* you refine your ability to *recognize and compare categories* of experience (past and present), and you astutely sift from your experiences the *essential similarities, differences, and essential organizing principles* that will allow you to more accurately interpret the likely outcomes of your choices and behaviors, while interacting with the circumstances and challenges you face.

Your life is a dynamic laboratory of cyclical hypotheses, experimentation, observations, analyses, conclusions, and adjustments—all derived from what happens to you and how you interpret these events. Your brain is an incredibly powerful instrument that records and processes experiences. A well-functioning brain learns from successes and failures and forms associations that cumulatively track and avoid past mistakes and generalize to new situations bearing resemblance to previous experiences and successful responses. Your brain also has a marvelous "hard drive" with random access to billions of memories. An intact brain that learns well and acts responsibly and profitably must be *flexible*—it must rely upon habit and efficiency, but allow for perception of subtle and vital similarities and differences between situations you've been in before and the present ones you are facing.

This may sound complicated, but it just describes the regime you normally follow throughout a typical day. You employ these cognitive skills and principles in routine activities, ranging from what, when, and how you eat, to how you plan your work and schedule, and also what you expect and how you behave with cooperative or difficult people.

For instance, if you have food allergies or sensitivities, you are vigilant to avoid certain foods. If you've had food poisoning, you're more careful about not eating what you believe made you sick. Healthy and vulnerable people learn to "put two and two together." Individuals vary, but most of us eventually track down and discover that eating certain substances in some quantities at particular times (e.g., spicy foods, large amounts, late at night, before exercising, etc.) make us quite uncomfortable; thus we tend to avoid repeating what led to the unpleasant outcome. The same goes for eating in particular restaurants whose food may taste good but may produce undesirable consequences. (And sometimes it requires many trials to change the behavior.)

This is the essence of using probability to assess risk and benefit. You review what happened before in similar circumstances, and you make informed and strategic choices based upon past results and projection of future outcomes.

The food example is simple and pedestrian; but the implications and ramifications of using past experiences to predict future ones and guide behaviors accordingly are vast.

Transportation agencies, engineers, meteorologists, and pilots assess risk in navigation and make key decisions that can have life or death implications. Keen students adjust study habits based on previous tests and grades. Doctors and pharmacists weigh research and benefits of medications against side effects and contraindications. We all form categories of experience that enable us to predict outcomes more reliably and thus guide us in making decisions. Our experiential categories filter our interpretations of new experiences according to how much they resemble predecessors and what we can do to influence outcomes in our favor.

You may argue with your spouse or partner in ways that have history. You know the provoking comments and their ensuing retorts, the uncannily predictable repetition of emotional escalation, and the likely unsatisfactory outcomes. In these situations (as in so many others), the old adage applies: *If you keep doing more of what you're doing, you're likely to end up with more of what you got.*

In a nutshell, probability in real life means assessing risks and costs and predicting benefits and likely results, both vicariously and with your own experiences.

Let's see how these concepts apply to everyday life.

Moving From Lab to Field

We are all creatures of habit. We are "learning organisms," and we rely upon structure, habit, routine, and predictability to organize our behaviors and anticipate consequences. Here are some examples of how probability blends and assists us in using other principles to get more of what we want:

EXAMPLE 1:

SELF–DISCIPLINE AND ROUTINE

I've noticed that certain "tricks" reliably help me avoid overeating and eating sweets. These propensities combine probability with frequency and duration to keep me satisfied and sustainable on a dietary regimen I determined is better for me.

I know I sleep better and feel better the next morning when I go to bed on less than a full stomach. I also know that the more sweets and carbs I eat, the more I tend to want. So I take advantage of certain techniques to tilt the odds in my favor (with regard to nature, whose daunting and relentless forces keep me challenged!).

If I eat moderate amounts of quality protein and fat before my blood sugar dips, I become satisfied with small portions and few or no carbs. If I eat less and eat earlier in the evening, I rest and feel better. If I avoid sweets, my desire for them dwindles in proportion to how much and how often I eat them. These are all observations I made reliably over time about how my own behaviors with food influence my desired and logistical outcomes.

These observations are also intertwined with frequency, duration, and probability. The less frequently I stuff myself or eat unhealthy foods, the less I *want* them. (There is definitely a scientific nutritional relationship here; but in this example I'm emphasizing the *correlative observation.*) It may seem counterintuitive—but I feel less deprived the less often and the longer I go without indulging myself.

As I indulge less frequently, the probability that I will indulge decreases (a good thing). To boot, the longer I go without indulging or eating in excess, the more likely it is that this habit will establish itself as the new normal, and the easier it is for me to continue a healthy pattern. I found that eating ice cream (because I "deserve" it) just leads to wanting more ice cream the next day. Consider that, once in a while, ice cream is okay. But for me, *thinking about it* requires too much stress and work. I need my physiology to cooperate and make life easier. I have lots of ice cream in my freezer (multiple favorite flavors). I eat ice cream once every few months or less frequently. I love ice cream, but it's a wicked tempter, and the habit of abstinence simply works better for me.

I found that when I exit from the kitchen (where I usually relax after dinner) and go upstairs, my desire for dessert drops dramatically. It's uncanny how I can think about and crave dessert in one room, but twenty steps upstairs and brushing my teeth eradicates my desire for more food, including carbs! Funny coincidence, but I capitalize on it.

Additionally I noticed that eating a handful of grapes or berries satisfies my sweet tooth and eliminates the craving for processed or high-sugar foods. Though there's a nutritional underpinning for that effect, the message here is that I can positively change the probabilities surrounding my eating behaviors by strategic observations and cause-and-effect interventions.

Probabilities are similarly influential and modifiable concerning my exercise. The more hours that elapse during the day, the less likely I am to exercise. Even if I have more time later in the day, I am unlikely to exercise. If I'm going to work out, I better do it early in the day—or else, it rarely happens. Therefore, I follow the habit and plan and execute my gym visits earlier. This leads to more frequency, greater intensity, and longer duration of exercise. After I exercise, almost always feel much better! This spirals into a habit of higher probability that I will exercise regularly.

Observation and habit are great companions to reinforce the company of success and confidence if you treat them with respect and garner their wisdom.

AVOIDING & MINIMIZING CONFLICT & NEGATIVE INTERACTIONS

Throughout life, we all have to deal with people who give us a hard time. There are those who thrive on conflict, many whose habits or personalities are annoying, and some who appear downright hostile or actively or passively aggressive.

For some, conflict and/or toxic relationships are constant and oppressive. If you associate (or live) with an angry, manipulative, unsympathetic, or narcissistic person, you know very well how difficult it is to keep the peace and interact productively with them. Some people just know how to "get your goat." Indeed they can even thrive on it.

However, you can judiciously use the probability principle to greatly reduce conflict and negative interactions. Even if you can't reform the person giving you grief, you can make choices and behave in ways that improve the chances you'll take the high road in dealing with negativity and conflict, and feel good about yourself in so doing so. The vindicating aspect of this tactic is that you can do this regardless of your antagonist's reactions.

Whether you face a personal attack on your integrity, a rude or inattentive service provider, or an oppositional person who distorts reality and blames you, it's possible to routinely emerge from such interactions with a calm nervous system, preserved dignity and self-esteem, and a sense of winning through acting respectably and minimizing conflict and loss. Oftentimes, simply shortening the interaction with someone bent on dragging you down is a victory.

The key to accomplishing such outcomes lies in keenly observing the consistency of negative outcomes and the probability of such continuation if you repeat the same responses and overtures. Said plainly, difficult people have a way of trapping you into repeating the same logical statements that fall on deaf ears. They also have a way of pushing emotional buttons so that, before you know it, you lose your equanimity and self-control. You've probably reviewed and analyzed these situations dozens of times, only to become frustrated with how little sense it all makes.

The only practical way to "figure out" such dysfunction is to observe and work with the probabilities involved—that is, the strikingly high chance that *if you keep doing more of what you're doing, you're likely to end up with more of what you got*. And trust me: the other guy will keep doing more of what he's done before!

To change the outcome, you must do something different. What? Hard to say with regard to a specific situation—but here are some guidelines:

a) Enter the interaction determined to act differently than you have previously with this person and in this type of conflict. The new angle you try may not work great, but the probability is on your side that it will work better than what you've done before. Change in inertia favors the initiator.

b) *Observe the outcome carefully*. The new behavior you try may not seem better or more logical, but it may result in movement toward what you want.

c) Focus on minimizing your responses, both emotional and substantive. Say less, and don't show intense or animated feelings. It's fine to verbalize your feelings (even distressed feelings)—just don't act them out. No yelling or raising your voice, no nonverbal expressions of contempt.

d) Focus on damage control. Some people simply don't know how to negotiate or compromise. With them, minimizing the interaction and cutting your losses can be a major win. Especially with people who are bent on dominating or manipulating, leaving the interaction—and with people who are not dear or influential in your life, leaving the relationship—is the very smart action.

e) Evaluate how your newer actions affected the outcome. By carefully observing cause and effect between your actions and the results (regardless of your adversary's rigidity), you can find how changes in your reactions help you take control and considerably alter the probability of better outcomes in your favor.

The zebra may not change his stripes, but you don't have to argue with or get trampled by him. Use the tools of probability and objective observation to modify the frequency, intensity, and duration of your conflicts and negative interactions.

EXAMPLE 3:

ACCELERATING LEARNING

As with most behaviors, learning new things becomes a function of habit. The more you practice the right ways, the more ingrained, easy, and even automatic the tasks become.

The contributions of frequency, intensity, and duration to the assimilation and accommodation of new knowledge and skills are vital. The previous chapters that dealt with these principles give you a head start toward implementing successful strategies. You can now add the probability principle to the mix, and make it your ally in accelerating your learning.

Among the challenges and impediments in learning and mastering new material and skills are: stress, avoidance, procrastination, confusion, feelings of embarrassment, inadequacy, or failure, and insufficient baseline knowledge or requisite past experience.

Learning new material (concepts and/or "how-to" skills) requires practice of the correct behaviors and their components. Whether you try to learn new math, fix or build something, learn a program, or coordinate a team or a better organizational plan for doing things, there are probabilities that you should consider and factor into your game plan.

In learning and practicing new behaviors, you can use frequency, intensity, and duration to observe and quantify your behaviors; then use these observations, along with the principles that govern them, to modify your *habits* and *schedules* (patterns of behavior), incorporating probability to increase behaviors you want and decrease those you don't want.

For example, you may find that you just don't have enough time in your day to devote to new learning activities, avoid distractions, and spend the time necessary to get everything done. Or you may become tired and stressed at the end of the day, and just not have the energy or desire to work on attaining your short- and long-term goals or fulfilling your daily responsibilities. By *observing* how you react and progress through the day, you gain valuable information about how to alter the probabilities of follow-through and success in your favor.

For me, the probability of exercising is highest between midmorning and late afternoon. Although this is inconvenient for my work schedule, I simply find that as the day progresses toward dinnertime, the probability that I will exercise (much less enjoy it) diminishes drastically. So I know that the probability of my exercising is higher during the middle of the day. This observation makes it easier to establish and reinforce this habit. For mental activities, I am at my best and most eager to write and dispatch administrative tasks early in the morning. My best creative moments are at night (even while I am sleeping). I go to bed with lots of ideas germinating in my mind; when I awaken, I am fresh, ready to write them down, and organize my ideas effectively. When I get a novel and appealing idea, I always make a few notes—the probability that I'll follow up on these notes and expand upon them is quite high; whereas if I fail to jot notes, the ideas often get away from me.

Thus by watching my behaviors and yielding to my habits of schedule, I greatly increase the probability that I will create, organize, and follow through. By using observation to navigate probability, the job of "forcing myself" is almost entirely that of self-observation and going with my own flow.

You may find that certain tasks just elude you, or you avoid them. Chances are that if you observe your tendencies and schedules, you can manipulate the frequency, intensity, and duration of your "new learning" work habits to increase the probability that you will practice more consistently and effectively.

Getting ahead often requires a combination of planning, perseverance, careful observation, and the keenness to "ride the horse in the direction it's going."

EXAMPLE 4:

REDUCING UNWANTED BEHAVIORS

Getting rid of unwanted behaviors is among the most difficult of tasks. Strong scientific and practical reasons support this. (If you are interested in finding out more about the science and practice of modifying behaviors, please see the extensive descriptions in my book, *Living Intact: Challenge and Choice in Tough Times*). In a nutshell, it's much easier to shape behaviors into habit (that is, form, increase, and strengthen behaviors) than it is to reduce or eliminate them. This is due to the nature and power of reinforcement.

Reinforcement is the process by which a consequence follows a behavior (and is associated with that behavior) such that the effect of the consequence upon the behavior is to increase or maintain the behavior's *frequency, intensity, or duration*. Sound familiar? In other words, reinforcement increases the likelihood that a behavior will reoccur. Notice how instrumentally probability is threaded throughout nature!

The problem with reducing behaviors intentionally (assuming they are unwanted) is that whenever we pay any kind of attention to a behavior (even just noticing or acknowledging it), we reinforce that behavior (albeit inadvertently). The kicker is that unwanted or nuisance behaviors elicit our attention, despite our strongest efforts to ignore them. It's a catch-22.

Now I offer a practical way out of this trap that is easy to do, and it almost always works. Before understanding the detail, remember that the *secret to reducing unwanted behaviors is to stop reinforcing them*. But because this is so hard to do, you need a viable alternative that allows you to reinforce what you want, instead of what the other person or the environment manipulates you into reinforcing.

Let's use a common example of a child's disruptive behavior. Suppose you have a child who is constantly seeking or demanding attention by certain undesirable behaviors (e.g., complaining, screaming tantrums, acting out, provoking others, general misbehavior.) Rather than react to the behavior (yes, certainly out-of-bounds behavior must be sanctioned and stopped . . . but look where that leads—reinforcement and eventual strengthening of those very behaviors), you might try the following:

a) Assess a baseline for several time periods in which the behavior occurs regularly.

b) For example, you might observe and record that the child disrupts or acts out several times per hour.

c) From your baseline, *estimate* how long the child is likely to go before committing a transgression. You do this by using the data from your observations. For instance, your sampling observations might show you that the child seems able to go fifteen minutes at a time with good behavior, but rarely goes more than thirty minutes without doing something objectionable.

d) Assign probability values in terms of percentages to short periods of time corresponding to "good behavior" (absence of transgressions).

e) For example, the probability that the child can go five minutes without a transgression may be 90 percent; the probability that he goes fifteen minutes may be 80 percent; and the probability that he goes twenty-five minutes without a transgression is 10 percent. As you can see (or graph), as time without or between transgressions increases, the probability of continued good behavior decreases. Thus you have a predictability model, using probabilities estimated from your observations.

f) Schedule a positive reinforcement somewhere around the 80 percent probability that good behavior continues. That is, deliberately intervene and reward the "good behavior," which is the absence of misbehavior or disruptiveness. Using the example above, you would reward the child at approximately every fifteen-minute interval during which he did not misbehave.

g) The reason for this is that people tend to learn most effectively at a reinforcement rate somewhere around 80 percent. Above that success rate, the person feels good, but little new learning or improvements occur. As the reinforcement probability drops, the challenge becomes too great and discouragement ensues, while motivation and effort decrease.

h) As the child compiles more rewards and successes in going fifteen-minute intervals without misbehaving, you can gradually lengthen the intervals, leading him to go longer and longer periods without misbehaving. The increased *duration* is often imperceptible to the child (better performance does not seem like extra effort), but you will definitely notice it.

This method uses probability as a guideline to successfully reinforce and *shape* behaviors that are *incompatible* with the undesirable behaviors that you do not want to reinforce. By focusing attention and systematic intervention on what you do want, you avoid the trap of reacting to and reinforcing what you don't want.

When moving pianos, you use pulleys (elevators) and low-friction mats. When moving behaviors, you sneak through the back door by making probability your ally.

If you like this example and want more explanation and methods for "skinning the cat a different way, " read my example of the gym shorts and string in Chapter 5 of *Living Intact: Challenge and Choice in Tough Times.*

DEVELOPING PREDICTION MODELS

Probability involves prediction, the mathematical calculation of the likelihood that something will occur. As described earlier, we use probability constantly, usually without even noticing that we are assessing what might happen based upon what has happened before in similar circumstances.

You can use probability consciously in very powerful ways to steer yourself away from actions and situations that may harm or disappoint you. Probability will also help you choose actions that will lead to successful and pleasing outcomes a high percentage of the time. In order to make probability your ally, you need to develop models of prediction to guide you.

You don't need fancy formulas or computer programs to improve upon your predictions and to utilize them for savvy guidance. You do need to develop the habit of keen *objective observation*. For some people, this comes more easily than for others. Observing objectively means gathering and recording (by memory and/or in writing) perceptions and facts about events, influences, and circumstances. Obviously, all of us observe and record on a continuing basis, as we live and interact with the world.

A familiar obstacle to objectivity is that we have a stake in the way things turn out. We are usually *invested* in outcomes (often without our realizing it). This subjectivity and emotional investment is natural; however, it can interfere by substituting the way we want things to be, rather than seeing them the way they really are. Thus we tend to project our desires or expectations on the interpretation of events.

For instance, if you decide to track the number of distractions that keep you from getting more done, you might tend to "overlook" events that intrude, by discounting or justifying them (e.g., having to respond to interruptions or emergencies; sudden ideas about what you remember you must do; breaking news that erupts across media and grabs attention; unexpected phone calls or emails, etc.). While any of these examples might be "justified," they still count as distractions—and they add up.

We filter things, rationalize, and make excuses: "I haven't eaten today." (Meaning I haven't had a meal; those handfuls of nuts, chips, and that beverage don't count.) "I only yelled at my family member because I was stressed and didn't sleep well."

This tendency to justify, project, and override facts interferes with the ability to make predictions and modifications based upon recent history.

So how can you counter the common predisposition to subjectivity in order to become more objective and effective? Here are several suggestions:

1. **Write things down.**

    We tend to believe we will remember things because they seem so clear or important at the time they occur. Even if we don't "forget" them, events blur and combine with succeeding experiences, and our brains *accommodate* them to fit with what we already know, think, and feel. Simply writing down your impressions briefly, at the time you observe events, will give you a record *and* a "memory jog" to remind you of what you actually observed.

    Consider the statement: *Black and white in print is much clearer and more distinct than the gray matter in the brain.*

2. **Perform simple analyses.**

    You may have calculated your car's miles per gallon by noting the trip odometer mileage since your last gas tank fill-up. Dividing this number by the number of gallons you pump into your car (assuming you do this from full tank to full tank after you drive the number of miles) will give you the average number of miles your car gets per gallon. It's an easy analysis that gives a reliable estimate.

You can perform such simple analyses on your own behavior, the behavior of others, and your interactions with them. For instance, suppose you want to get the attention of your boss (or husband, or child). You hesitate and feel inhibited because your previous experience tells you that this person is usually occupied, and either ignores you or expresses subtle resistance or unreceptiveness to your overture. You might try keeping a simple log of different times you approached this person, along with a rating of the person's response to you.

The different times categories might be:

1. when he finishes a phone call
2. after he returns from the restroom
3. when you see him smiling
4. when he pauses from what he's been doing

Ratings might be:

1. ignores you
2. looks up with slight annoyance
3. acknowledges you (says, "Yes," or What?"), but body language says "I wish you wouldn't interrupt me."
4. Tells you to go away
5. Smiles and welcomes you

Once you have some data, you can better determine at what times and under what conditions (the other person's activity) you stand a higher chance of being welcomed instead of facing a cool reaction.

3. **Track and verify trends and reliability.**
   In the car mileage example, you may want to repeat the mileage estimate a few times to gain reliability. If you are

watching other people's behavior (and your own), you need some repetition (additional data), perhaps with varying conditions, to begin seeing trends that support more accurate predictions. Thus you can use this information to adjust your expectations and behavior accordingly.

Once you practice monitoring and tracking discrete observable behaviors in the environment, you can expand to monitoring and tracking your internal behaviors—that is, how thoughts and feelings occur in repetitive cycles and associate themselves with each other and with what you do. You will be amazed and enlightened by the extent to which you are driven by strong emotions, especially negative ones. You will see in detail how fears, anxieties, and negative forecasts influence your actions. By observing and then vanquishing negative emotions, you can greatly increase your probability of executing carefully chosen behaviors to maximize successful outcomes. (For guidelines and instructions on eliminating negative emotions, see my book, *Living Intact: Challenge and Choice in Tough Times.*)

4. **Separate your emotional attachment from the evidence.** The hallmark of good science is objectivity. That doesn't mean you don't care about outcomes. It means you separate your emotional investments and attachments from factual data. This is not easy, but it can be done as a matter of routine when you have systematic controls and methods in place.

   You don't need a laboratory; you just need your brain and consistent practice observing events, recording data and trends, and minimizing interpretations until you have sufficient evidence to corroborate your hypotheses and interpretations.

5. **Reinforce yourself for following these steps.**

It always helps to "pat yourself on the back" for small successive steps in the right direction. Recognizing and highlighting your positive steps will do more than make you feel good. It will raise the probability that you will keep implementing the tactical observational strategies that underpin increasing success.

To begin reinforcing yourself in this process, make a list of several incidents per day in which you observed behaviors and how the conditions under which they occur increase or decrease the likelihood they will occur again.

I make a daily habit of taking stock of my productive interactions with people—notably, encounters in which I helped someone, made a person feel good about himself, expressed compassion and understanding (thereby connecting with someone emotionally), and minimized the fallout and risk from toxic people and negative interactions.

When you adopt and shape this habit, you will become very empowered!

TESTING HYPOTHESES ABOUT BEHAVIOR

A hypothesis is a proposed explanation for a phenomenon—a theory needing support from empirical investigation. Essentially, a hypothesis is a formal hunch.

We make hypotheses all the time—conjecturing and anticipating what will happen. Our expectations are based partly on verified experience, partly on hope and faith and partly on desires. The contributions of each of these factors relate to how grounded we are in material reality. In order to test hypotheses about behaviors, we must use an organized system, such as the scientific method.

The scientific method is a body of techniques for investigating phenomena, acquiring new knowledge, or correcting and integrating previous knowledge. To be termed scientific, a method of inquiry is commonly based on empirical or measurable evidence subject to specific principles of reasoning.

You don't need a scientific team or a laboratory to test your own hypotheses about behavior and use your conclusions to formulate predictions. Hone your skills of observation and subject them to the scrutiny of objectivity.

As you collect information about cause and effect between events in any particular circumstances, activities, and relationships, you will become better at using the accuracy of your predictions to assess probabilities. With this evolving information, you can stack the odds of winning in your favor by choosing certain courses of action, while avoiding others.

A simple example comes to mind: sometimes I become apprehensive that what I depend on won't continue to go well. Though I'm not obsessive, I do occasionally worry that my stream of income could dwindle, my wife might become disinterested, or my health may deteriorate. While none of these things have happened so far, that's not to say they couldn't. I reassure myself by examining the trends in my life—recent and past history, consistency, and my own motivations. Although there are no guarantees, my objective observations and analyses lead me to conclude that things will probably continue along the good paths that have been established. Such evidence-based observation and reasoning gives me reassurance, confidence, and purpose to persist in what has so far worked.

On the other hand, using probability and objective analysis deters me from continuing to pursue fruitless or counterproductive methods out of habit or sheer doggedness. You know the saying, *If you keep doing more of what you're doing, you'll likely get more of what you've got.*

A punchier way of expressing this concept goes like this: *The definition of insanity is doing the same thing over and over again, but expecting different results.*

Probability is one of the key principles that helps us take charge and get ahead. Life is full of chance, serendipity and—yes—miracles. There is much beyond our control. Yet the math and logic of probability can greatly assist organizing our experience, inferences, and choices to make the heads-up modifications that make us come out on top.

Though life is full of gambles, we can use probability wisely to reduce risks and raise our percentage of winning bets. Don't be foolish about or afraid of chance. Take charge of it.

"Chances are that if your parents didn't have children, you won't either."

—Anonymous

CHAPTER 6

CONTEXT

Interpret And
Organize Reality

Along the path to maturity, wisdom, and the many benefits of experience, we must acquire the capacity to put things into perspective. This means interpreting and organizing events, thoughts, feelings, knowledge, and new information into realistic and useful representations and patterns. The organization and categorization of information must have recognizable reference points and connections with other valid parts of experience. These connections, interrelationships, perspectives, and reference points comprise *context*.

Context is the principle that helps us see both the larger and smaller picture aspects, how parts relate to the whole, and how the pieces of life fit together. Context weaves and integrates information, concepts, and experience so that they are:

1. consensually or similarly perceived and understood by others;

2. appropriately related to the connecting circumstances in which they are viewed; and

3. conducive to making sense in the surrounding conditions in which they occur.

Context serves as the background that helps identify, locate, understand, and interpret information. For example, if I tell you the information "150 pounds" in isolation, it's difficult to interpret what that means. However, if I say, "The dog weighs 150 pounds," you know it's a big dog. If I say, "The seven-year-old girl weighs 150 pounds," you know that the child is quite overweight. If I say, "The man was six feet, three inches tall, and weighed 150 pounds," you can picture a skinny man.

Consider the question, "What is the right speed to drive?"

Of course, a good answer is context sensitive. The "right speed" depends on the conditions, many of which are often changing. Sixty-five miles an hour may be the right speed to drive on the highway, but certainly not on a residential street. If traffic on the highway is bumper-to-bumper, then a much slower speed is appropriate in that circumstance.

Hence the *context* in which information or events appear contributes essentially to what they mean. We use context clues continually to make sense of things, to organize experience, and to select interpretations and actions. In language communication, we use context to determine the proper semantic usage of the same words that can have different meanings and even different pronunciations.

CONTEXT IN LANGUAGE

For instance:

- The word *read* can be a present tense verb (pronounced *reed*) or a past tense verb (pronounced *red*).

- The word *bark* can mean what a dog does, or it can mean the skin of a tree.

- The word *tear* can mean to rip apart, or it can mean a drop of moisture formed in the eye.

- *Left* can mean the opposite of right, or it can mean gone away.

- *Stalk* can mean to follow/harass someone, or it can mean a part of a plant.

- *Old* can mean previous or occurring earlier, or it can mean aged.

Consider this sentence: *Fighting bullies can be dangerous.*

The grammar and linguistic deep structure of this simple sentence is ambiguous. It can be interpreted in two ways:

1. Bullies who fight can be considered as dangerous people.

2. To fight a bully can be a dangerous activity.

Notwithstanding linguistic structure and rules, language context can be confusing. As such, it is often the basis for hilarious comedy and verbal pranks upon unsuspecting listeners. A more common usage of a word or phrase, when paired with surrounding words in a sudden change of context, acquires a completely different and humorous meaning:

"Now, take my wife . . . PLEASE!" —Henny Youngman

"When I was a kid, my parents bought me a mood swing set." —Steven Wright

Whether or not you are fond of language and feel comfortable with nuances and word games, counterpoints in language present many examples of the ways in which context can aid, distort, clarify, or confuse the meanings and sensibilities of communications and situations. Remember the infamous statement by President Bill Clinton when he was questioned about his "unpresidential" activities regarding Monica Lewinsky?

Contending that his statement that "there's nothing going on between us" was truthful in that he had no ongoing relationship with Lewinsky at the time he was questioned, when he said, "It depends upon what the meaning of the word 'is' is."

In presenting these examples, my purpose is not to mire you in linguistic complexities; rather it is to give examples of the influence of *context* on interpreting reality and shaping perception. The effects of context often trigger feelings, determine decisions, shape expectations and motivation, and lead to courses of action.

Context is a critical foundation that determines how influential and effective the other six principles explained in this book will be in helping you take charge and control of your desired outcomes.

We will examine how context interacts with these principles and how you can incorporate context into your arsenal of tools for life control.

But first take another look at some remarkable "sleight-of-hand" effects of context:

THE DIPLOMA

When a student complained about the way his name appeared on his diploma, which read: JOHN DASINDOG SMITH, the registrar replied that the diploma was printed exactly as the student had requested. In rebuttal, the student demanded that the diploma be reprinted correctly. He repeated again that his name was "John D. (as in 'dog') Smith."

If you, dear reader, walked right into that one, you are not alone. By way of apology for the trick, feel free to share this liberally. It can fool almost everyone. Ask someone to read the name aloud, and you will surely hear what you first read. People with dyslexia hold no dominion over such sleight of vision and linguistics.

Aside from its clever trickery, the John Smith example illustrates the power of *context* in shaping the perception of *content*. We see and hear what is most obvious and in keeping with our conditioning, preferences, and comfort zones. We accept what fits our models of the world, while filtering out the complex or inconvenient. We hear what we want or expect to hear—mostly—and we look for validation.

There is something to be said for having a point of view and not being double-minded or addled by exotic fads. Maturity carries with it the virtue of time-tested wisdom. Be wary however, that a narrow mindset may saddle you with the middle name of DASINDOG, a peculiar distinction. The message is that we must see both—the forest and the trees, the big and the little pictures, each in their turn—and be able to shift and switch between them as appropriate and useful.

Content and context are both distinct and integrated, like lyrics and melody, phrasing and rhythm. When we shift attention from one to the other, the message and feeling can change.

CONTEXT ALLOWS FOR FLEXIBILITY

The larger concept surrounding my language examples is again about context (rather than the vagaries of pronunciation and syntax). The language examples depending upon context illustrate the need for *flexibility* in adjusting to the situation. Life requires flexibility, and life provides repeated lessons and opportunities to attain greater mastery in exercising and applying flexibility. Flexibility allows us to incorporate new information, combine new data with existing knowledge and experience, and shift gears to react appropriately to constantly changing conditions.

This process occurs continuously at the internal level of body-and-mind functions as well as in the ways we interact with the world. Flexibility lets us hone in on details to discern important attributes and nuances. Flexibility also allows us zoom out to apprehend the bigger picture and appreciate the integration of parts and whole.

We all need a well-functioning "zoom lens"—a mental ability that adjusts to the near and the far, and practices doing so fluidly, seamlessly. Without such capacity, experiences may seem confusing and frustrating. In a music ensemble, each instrument played well contributes; they must be practiced individually, and then orchestrated to get the full and pleasing, synergistic effect.

I can identify with the misunderstood John Smith (as described above). Yet many times, I've been frustrated by "John Smith situations" when, so set in my ways, I've missed the obvious. Life is more fluid and rewarding when I can shift my mindset to see more than one point of view. Interestingly, exercising that flexibility feels yielding and empowering rather than stressful or complicated. Whenever I think I know all the answers, I remind myself to check to see if I've asked the right questions.

The Hebrew word *shalom* means both "goodbye" and "hello." Shalom can also mean "peace" or "harmony." The Russian word *pajalste* means both "please" and "thank you," as well as "here you are" and "you're welcome." In Chinese, the symbols for the word "crisis" mean both "problem" and "opportunity." Context determines semantics and interpretation.

UNDERSTANDING CONTEXT

Context indicates the setting or framework that helps to structure and interpret information and events. Context is key to understanding and organizing experience as well as constructing cohesive and sensible patterns of reality.

Think of context as a tool or instrument that helps us transition from the small picture to the big picture, to see the whole as more or different than a collection or sum of parts.

Ascertaining context allows the "fitting together" of things into patterns, relationships, and time sequences that organize experience and help us function.

Determining context facilitates:

- generalizing from examples to concepts or trends;
- encouraging motivation;
- helping to calm anxieties;
- developing perseverance;
- crystallizing and maintaining vision of goals;
- assessing the behaviors, habits, and motivations of others;
- resolving ambiguities; and
- analyzing cause and effect and predicting outcomes.

APPLICATIONS OF CONTEXT

When using context in conjunction with other Life Control principles, you take into consideration factors such as surrounding circumstances, special and changing conditions, and evolving variables to make adequate assessments and useful decisions. For instance, a key concept in using context is that of determining whether an individual's behavior is *in character* or *out of character* with what you know about that person.

When someone behaves *in character*, he is acting in a manner consistent with his patterns of previous behavior. People tend to repeat their behaviors. A person who is frequently late is likely to be late again. Thus instances of tardiness are in character for that person. On the other hand, when someone who is rarely late doesn't show up on time, it may be cause for concern; or, at the very least, you might anticipate a reason for lateness that is unusual and not simply another excuse (as might be expected from the person who is habitually late).

In-character behaviors are likewise established and demonstrated through repetition. While they are not infallible, the patterns serve as good predictors for behavior and their associated setting of expectations. Someone who offers to pick up the check or pay another's way will often make that same gesture. People who are stingy or cautious with money will likely reveal thrift or prudence in multiple financial situations.

Argumentative people cause conflict. Peacekeepers try to avoid conflict and seek compromise and concessions. Predictions about their responses in new situations may be reliably inferred from their previous patterns of reactions.

Out-of-character behaviors are those *atypical of* or *inconsistent with* a person's usual pattern. When a person who is ordinarily lively or excitable presents as muted or flat, you suspect that something is wrong. When a punctual person doesn't show up or notify you, you may become worried. When your normally hungry pet doesn't eat, there is cause for concern.

The message is this: when you carefully assess a person's *in-character* and *out-of-character* behaviors, you develop a context for anticipating actions and emotions and for planning your own behavioral responses. By expecting certain responses (based on a previous track record), you are not blindly stereotyping people. Rather you are using contexts for accommodating their responses and planning and adjusting your own. This assumes of course that you have reasonably accurate and reliable data from your experiences and observations.

In using context to predict behaviors based on character, you are essentially employing the principle and power of probability, modified by contextually sensitive influential factors. Context can be critical for sensibly implementing other principles, including frequency, duration, and intensity. For instance, ramping up your exercise routine by manipulating these variables can be modified if needed when you are sick or injured.

Adjustments in diet and time schedules may also be suitable to periodic reflection your current health status, the needs of others, and time-sensitive circumstances. Visiting a sick friend or relative, interrupting your preferred routines to help someone, granting yourself some temporary indulgence under deadlines or extenuating circumstances are examples of the need for flexibility, taking into account the context in which your ordinary or preferred behaviors may occur.

Context is used in making all kinds of social, judicial, and financial assessments and decisions. Legal convictions and sentences usually consider a defendant's past history of infractions. Lawyers striving for opposing determinations deliberately present information in carefully constructed contexts to influence the interpretations and judgments. Lenders make decisions based upon considerations of debts, income, length of employment, interest rates, etc.

The longevity and importance of relationships often depend upon context to sway decisions and behavioral persistence. Long-term marriages, finances, health, and family needs are variables that exert strong influences on how one copes with the impact of adversity or dashed expectations.

Context also plays a role in decision-making with regard to health. Your willingness to accept the risks of medications or surgeries must be balanced with the risks and probabilities associated with your diagnosed conditions.

As athletes and sports spectators know, constantly shifting game and competition factors drive moves and decisions according to the time, score, opposition, conditions, and relative importance of the situation. Borrowing and spending money can be wiser or more foolish, depending upon many factors that comprise context. In hindsight, most of us have experienced "buyer's remorse" or "what was I thinking?" in regard to regretted purchases. On the other hand, borrowing to buy property or finance college may be a wise investment, depending upon many factors.

How much you spend (and in what circumstances) can be heavily influenced by sales, bargain deals, and how much money or resources you have at given periods. Your motivation, intensity, frequency, and duration of working or studying is likely to be influenced by tests, deadlines, impeding visits, and the occurrence (in context) of other obligations, events, and commitments you have.

Context is a background part of everything we do. We don't often focus on context per se—we just automatically assimilate and process the surrounding circumstances, situational factors, and calculated probabilities in momentary and more carefully planned decisions. However, many people have difficulty in using context to advantage. Gaining and using perspective can be elusive; without this adaptation and flexibility, any stress, adversity, emotional overwhelm, and tunnel vision can be defeating.

DEVELOPING VERSATILITY WITH CONTEXT

With a better understanding of the role of context in gaining control and success, we turn to the matter of how you can become more adept and versatile in sensing and applying context. By realizing that context is integral to how we perceive events and organize our responses, we're already ahead in the honing of awareness and the sharpening of our skills.

To focus on context sensitivity with the purpose of increasing your flexibility and having more options available, consider the following guidelines:

1. **Observe, assimilate, accommodate, respond.**
   As is often a key to success, careful and accurate *observation* is critical. This develops with time and practice (assuming you are basically reality-oriented and intact). You

must be disciplined in separating emotions and investments (desired outcomes) from facts and occurrences.
This is the foundation of objectivity and science. *Assimilation* is the process of acquiring new data and information,
including sorting and storing it. Accommodation is the
process of organizing new information so that it corre-
sponds with your existing *schema* for organizing reality.
Accommodation follows assimilation; they are both
natural cognitive processes we do constantly to organize
experiences and respond to the world.

2. **Assess potential outcomes.**
   While interpreting and planning your inner and outer
   responses to experiences, consider, and attempt to assess,
   the potential consequences and outcomes of various interpretations and responses. This doesn't necessitate dozens
   of meticulously calculated possibilities. It suggests that you
   assess the impact of your perceptions and actions.

   For instance, if someone owes you something and
   is not forthcoming (apologies, follow-through, money,
   etc.), you can role play in your mind the logical consequences of different positions: interpreting the person's
   behavior as *in character* for avoidance and irresponsibility,
   for example, may lead you to one set of actions with a
   probable and predictable outcome for that overture. De-
   ciding to be more patient and allow for possible reasons
   for the other person's behavior can more likely lead to a
   different response and anticipated outcome.

   Assessing potential outcomes viably and accurately
   incorporates the results of past experiences. Create the
   habit of asking yourself:

   ■ Have I faced situations with important similarities to
   the situation I'm facing now?

   ■ If so, what were the results of my actions? How did
   things turn out?

The context you choose will persuade you toward one course of action (and emotional response) versus another.

3. **Weigh costs and benefits.**
   Of course, you must weigh the costs and benefits associated with your choices of how to respond. The potential gains and losses are also context-sensitive in that you place certain values on the importance of each in given situations.

   Example: the cost of recovering money owed to you may not be worth the actual effort and bad will endemic to the process.

   Another example: in some situations, you may decide to set clear boundaries and make a point of certain limits in order to teach someone a lesson. Rescinding privileges or resources when someone repeatedly or defiantly refuses to comply may be consonant with a context of demonstrating that rules must be followed and that you mean what you say.

4. **Anticipate pressures, resistance, and pushback.**
   There's an old saying, "No one likes change except a wet baby." Overstated, perhaps, but the general idea that we tend to be set in our (comfortable) ways is true. When you force someone out of a comfort zone—even an irresponsible or dysfunctional one—you are likely to get resistance or pushback. This will put pressure on you to ease up, stand firm, or double down on your stand. The degrees of uncomfortable response (and your reactions to it) are context sensitive on both sides.

   The guideline of "choose your battles" is relevant here, as is the nature of context you associate with adversity or conflict. Sometimes "winning" goes beyond the immediate circumstance of personal gain, acquiescence, or the satisfaction of "being right." When you "stick to your guns" and prevail, it boosts your confidence and security in strategies for future encounters.

The other side of this coin is "winning the battle but losing the war." Perhaps a higher objective in many conflicts could be to hone your compromising and negotiating skills, establish good will and trust, and/or portray yourself as accommodating and flexible.

Contexts shed different lights, moods, and perspectives on circumstances with the same facts.

USING THE ZOOM LENS

The zoom lens metaphor is apt for the ability and practice to see the big picture and the details in a variety of situations. Our brains have vast abilities to process pattern recognition, details, and surrounding contexts; but we need to practice.

Whereas zooming in and zooming out occurs naturally as part of perception and cognitive processing, we can pay conscious attention to our habits of perceiving and analyzing situations and their attendant ambiguities. People have different and natural styles and preferences for honing in on details versus apprehending the larger picture. Some people are more global; others habitually focus in. Personal styles notwithstanding, we need to develop comfort and practice integrating each approach. Keeping a sense of the big picture is important (especially for context), but zooming in to inspect relevant details that matter and contribute to the general picture is also useful. (Your car or digital navigation device is a concrete visual example of the flexibility of different adjustable views.)

When your mental zoom lens works properly, you can integrate the here-and-now details and immediacy within the larger context of the history and potential future of your situation. Alternating and integrating the smaller and larger views enhances context by helping you put things in perspective. If you are struggling under intense pressure to pass exams or complete a boring and seemingly irrelevant course, the larger context (that you are working toward a degree and brighter future) can help your tolerance, motivation, and perseverance.

A push to meet a deadline, a tense meeting, or a work overload due to staff shortage (with the attendant overwork), may encumber you with stress and resentment. Seeing the longer-term picture of how the immediate demands relate to your integrity, habits, and goals goes a long way toward spurring your motivation and informed decisions (zooming out). Projecting inward from the bigger picture to the immediate details can provide the perspective and equanimity to stay the course for the sake of future outcomes (zooming in).

Sometimes, you have a limited sample of information from which to interpret and decide. A new friend, partner, or acquaintance may exhibit behaviors that concern you. Being late, lavish spending, overindulgence, and verbal insensitivity can all be warning signs of how this person will behave in the future. Projecting into the longer term from limited (but significant) current information is a way to use the zoom lens along with probability (prediction) and a consciousness of "in character versus out of character" evaluation to guide you in prudent decisions and actions.

IN CHARACTER VERSUS OUT OF CHARACTER

As mentioned previously, the concept of *in character* or *out of character* is a critical and practical guideline that helps place individual behavioral events in a useful context.

When evaluating someone's actions, determining whether an individual's behavior is *in character* or *out of character* regarding what you know about that person can be useful. When someone behaves *in character*, he is acting in a manner consistent with his patterns of previous behavior. People tend to repeat themselves. When someone does something atypical of his repertoire, it is *out of character* for that person.

You can also apply this differential to yourself. Do you occasionally respond by losing your cool? Do you become anxious or stressed when that's not usual for you? Are you typically excitable or unflappable?

Talkative or quiet? Quick to respond or more of a patient listener? By knowing your tendencies, you can judge whether certain reactions are *in character* or *out of character* for your, which can help you know when it's fitting to explain yourself to an audience who may be confused or disappointed when you react atypically.

For example: "Gee, John, I apologize for not getting back to you sooner; I've just been overwhelmed. But I have been thinking of you." Or: "I'm not very communicative lately, but it's not related to you. I've just been kind of stressed and self-absorbed."

Observing personal atypical behaviors in yourself (or having others point them out) may signal that you are under enormous stress or even becoming ill. Departures from similar behavior patterns within the same individuals can be important harbingers for action.

Out-of-character behaviors may call for forgiveness or ignoring mistakes. In-character behaviors help you plan and adjust your use of frequency, intensity, and duration, because you have reliable information about someone's probability of acting a certain way.

When communicating with others, we are constantly using frequency, intensity, and duration. Displays of talking, texting, emailing, and requests for meetings all tend to establish patterns. These patterns form the contexts by which we can anticipate and organize interactions with others.

A person who infrequently communicates or requests things from you may show an increased response, possibly indicating some stress or neediness. Alternatively, when someone who's regularly in contact checks out for a while, it can raise your antenna about whether something is wrong with that person or that some issue is occurring between you under the surface.

In situations involving family, social interactions, or business relationships, using the template of *in character* or *out of character* will help you interpret expected and unexpected behaviors in context so that you can adjust your perspective and responses accordingly. In-character behaviors represent high-probability responses; out-of-character behaviors represent low-probability responses. This knowledge helps you predict, plan, and adjust.

PERSONAL STYLE AND CONTEXT

You're likely aware of your personality characteristics, personal style, and behavioral tendencies. People get to know themselves over time. Though there are many components and characteristics of these traits and tendencies, for simplicity we can compare the styles of caution, careful adaptation to change, and measured, slower response with impulsiveness, quick decision-making, and comfort with change. Different styles represent contexts in which people will interpret others and their actions and weigh their own responses to and acceptance of a variety of behaviors.

Putting pressure on someone with a cautious response style will usually backfire in that it will make that person more resistant. Quick decision-makers who are comfortable with change and flux may respond more favorably to increased pressure (when presented in appropriate and nonthreatening language) because it feeds into their tendency and need to be decisive and attain closure.

According to your style, you should be informed and prepared regarding your mindset and tendencies to adapt in varying contexts. Knowing your excesses and downsides can help protect against the vulnerabilities of your style and comfort zone. For example, being overly cautious may hamper you if a situation calls for quick response. Too much delay or deliberation can foil opportunities. On the other hand, many situations are better handled by deliberation over time, doing further investigation or research, or shopping around for the best deal instead of making a hasty decision.

Life control principles are scientific and practical realities that operate reliably regardless of your style. However, knowing your preferences, go-to tendencies, and the influences over your judgment can help you more judiciously utilize context to make good decisions and implement tactics.

If you are unsure of your style or want help understanding more about yourself, contact a knowledgeable psychologist experienced in these assessment techniques. Such an investment will pay in successful dividends.

EMOTIONAL REGULATION, COGNITIVE PROCESSING, AND CONTEXT

As described, many factors and varying conditions can establish a surrounding context that influences perception and interpretation and can sway decisions and actions. Ingrained mindsets established through genetic predisposition, life experiences, and habits are the contexts that accompany patterns of emotional regulation and cognitive processing.

Though a significant percentage of the general population may be characterized with a style that is animated, active, enthusiastic, engaging, or excitable, an excess of this quality may constitute mania, hysteria, emotional lability, or overreactive mood swings. Alternatively, a temperament that is reserved, laconic, even dour can overreach into depression, resentment, hostility, and so forth. These pronounced stereotypes can become contexts that magnify perceptions and experiences to validate and conform to the prevailing internal cognitive and emotional set. Negative people expect things to go wrong. Positive people look for rewarding outcomes and silver linings.

We all filter happenings through the lenses of our familiar emotional and cognitive contexts. The value of this habit lies in accumulating data that support and confirm what we know to be true—just like solid scientific research establishes reliable findings. The disadvantage of practiced filters is that they interpret and affirm experiences that align with our biases, but which may actually signify conflicting meaning. We tend to misread or dismiss that which doesn't accrue to what we believe. Hence the saying, *The view looks different to an eagle than to a ground animal.*

Becoming aware of your own emotional and perceptual tendencies, your excesses and predilections, and your tendencies to affirm what you already believe is the case will help you be nimbler in recognizing context as the background for your assumptions, observations, and conclusions.

THE LETTER

A college student wrote the following to his parents:

> Dear Mom and Dad,
>
> It is with great regret and anxiety that I report to you some of my mistakes and troubles. I'm not doing well this semester; I'm getting two F's and had to drop two of my courses. I also had the misfortune of getting a DUI last week. And that girl whom I've been seeing . . . well, I really like her, and that's a good thing, because she just told me that she is pregnant.
>
> I'm sorry to disappoint you with this information. Actually, if any of it were true, I'd be quite ashamed. However, I just made this up to give you some perspective on how bad things could be. So, when I ask you for money (as I am now . . . PLEASE), hopefully you can put my need into perspective. Please send money!
>
> Love,
> Your son

MY OWN CONTEXT STORY

To highlight the idea that context adjustment is important in narrowing as well as widening the perspective, I share my own embarrassing story.

In 1981, I was living in Los Angeles. A physician who happened to be the son of my parents' friends was to visit Los Angeles, and my parents asked me to entertain him. Willingly, I took him to dinner and drove him around Hollywood and environs, showing him sights and landmarks. Unfortunately, I was pulled over for a traffic stop and ticketed for running a red light. Embarrassed and appalled, I determined to fight the citation because I had *not* run the light, but rather had stopped and reversed my car back a few feet, so passengers could cross. Livid about the citation, I nonetheless prepared to contest it.

To fortify my case, I asked my guest doctor to write a letter on my behalf attesting to witnessing that I did not run the light (which he did write on hospital letterhead). I went to traffic court and pleaded my innocence, presenting the doctor's letter as corroborating evidence.

The judge looked at the letter, then looked at me. He said, "Mr. Steinberg, you were not cited for running a red light. Look at your ticket: you were cited because your car extended into the crosswalk. You are an idiot, and I am dismissing your case."

In this irony, left with pride wounded, tail between my legs, I escaped the traffic violation, but not the cost to my ego and mortifying misperception. My certainty that I was innocent of a perceived charge overshadowed the necessary perspicacity to note important details.

Context is often the relevant determinant of what battle you're fighting.

CONTEXT IN COMBINATION WITH OTHER PRINCIPLES

Context is a critical foundation that determines how influential and effective the other six principles explained in this book will be in helping a person take charge and control their desired outcomes.

The effectiveness of other Life Control principles is facilitated by the appropriate use of context to reflect important situational variables and to adapt the techniques and tools of control to fit the surrounding circumstances and influencing factors. By itself, context helps you develop and maintain perspective, integrating the big and small pictures. Context becomes even more powerful however, when it underlies the implementation of other Life Control principles.

PRACTICE EXERCISE

List at least two examples of:

- Relationship conflicts or stresses;
- Self-management habit issues; and
- Ambitions, goals, and obstacles.

For each category, identify at least two different contexts that pro-vide different interpretations of and actions regarding the particular challenge.

CHAPTER 7

OSCILLATION

Repetition, Variation, and State

The principle of oscillation is part of Life Control because it underpins the workings of our natural universe, including our biological functioning and our behavior. Though oscillation is easily measured and displayed, we don't typically see or relate to it tangibly. It's easier to comprehend and monitor frequency, duration, intensity, and probability; because, although these are inferred concepts, we can assess them through monitoring our own behavior. If you pay attention, you know how intense something is, how long you do it, and how likely you are to engage in or witness a particular activity.

Oscillations occur and resonate continuously within and around us, but we typically need some instrument or external device to record or reflect them. You don't typically oscillate consciously; although with some training and keen observation, you can become attuned to differential rhythms that are pleasant or discordant. In addition to the oscillations that naturally comprise our nervous systems, sound and light waves, and electromagnetic energy, alignments and misalignments in oscillations that occur between individuals and other individuals correlate with how much "in tune" one perceives during experiences. The "vibes" you feel from another person or in a given situation are closely related to the alignments and patterns of oscillation in various energy forms. When you "click" or "jibe" with someone or something, or when you are feeling "in the zone," these states reflect particular patterns of oscillation in energy.

For practical use in gaining more control over your life, you don't need expertise in the scientific determinants of oscillation. However, a rudimentary acquaintance with this principle will help explain more about why we feel the various ways we do, what natural forces may affect our motivations, and some steps we can take to coerce the natural rhythms of oscillation to work better on our own behalf.

So bear with some technical explanation and detail in this chapter as groundwork to increase your awareness, understanding, and practical applications.

OSCILLATION AS A NATURAL PRINCIPLE

The natural universe is composed of many things that differ and many things that repeat themselves in duplication or close similarity. Some repetitions are exact replicas, and others are variations on a theme, recapitulations of essential organizing principles with slight discrepancies. You don't need a degree in physics to recognize this in everyday life. Patterns abound everywhere, from light patterns that make up colors to chemical compounds with different atomic structures that make up matter.

The patterns of repetition and variation that characterize the natural world also suffuse our human biological systems. Our organs secrete hormones, and our brains pump electrical signals that keep life processes flowing. These processes and patterns allow for the regulation and variations in biological systems and *states*. We naturally transition through different states in the course of each day. Sleep, for example, is a different state than waking consciousness. Of course, we each experience variable gradations of state, many on a regular basis. When things are flowing smoothly, we easily transition among states without much conscious attention. But sometimes, it's difficult to generate a state that adapts to the current conditions—such as not being able to gear down and fall asleep.

When the transitions between states are inefficient or obstructed, or when we become "locked in" a certain state (to the exclusion of other more appropriate states for the situation), we are likely to experience symptoms of distress, both physiological and psychological. People who are prone to excitable inner states often experience anxiety, agitation, or the various symptoms of trauma. Their brains and nervous systems reflexively launch into "fight-or-flight mode." After doing this for some time, the brain habituates to this state as "normal," which is actually not normal, except under conditions of threat or emergency.

The variations and continuations of state reflect patterns of fluctuations in the brain's electrical transmission called *oscillations*. An oscillation is a fluctuation or alternation back and forth. *Waveforms* that make up sound, light, and brainwave signals oscillate up and down in patterns. The greater the magnitude of the waveform, the higher the *amplitude*. The more "up-and-down" waveforms per second, the greater the *frequency*.

The pulses of electricity generated throughout our environment are oscillations that produce current. Thus the wavering or swinging back and forth, up and down of waveforms is the natural oscillation of energy endemic to the natural environment and to life.

We each experience these different oscillations as states in alertness, mood, and varying mental, emotional, and physiological responses. Sometimes they feel good and other times not so good. Our variations in oscillations and states may be deliberate, or they may be involuntary, as we respond to internal and external cues and influences. Anesthesia induces a change in state automatically, involuntarily. For many people, a situation or environmental stimulus, or even an intrusive thought may precipitate fear or anxiety. When you play a piece of music you like, you are deliberately inducing your brain to experience oscillations influenced by the auditory input of the music. Your brain changes—at least temporarily—to adapt to and copy the sound oscillations.

ASYNCHRONOUS AND SYNCHRONOUS OSCILLATION IN BRAIN ACTIVITY

Our brains function by means of neural impulses—billions of nerve cells fire through *action potentials* (brief pulses that travel down the neuron to excite yet other neurons). These nerve firings allow or inhibit transmission of information, including chemical and hormonal release, thus forming the control mechanisms and habits of the brain and nervous system. Our neurons are organized into *neural networks* (relay systems) that allow neural activity to organize itself into "cooperativity."

Brain activity may be accurately measured by engineering and physics principles that record the cycles of activity in terms of *frequency, amplitude,* and *phase relationships. Frequency* measures the number of wave cycles of the electrical activity from its highest point to its lowest point per second. A frequency of 10 Hz indicates electrical activity of ten cycles per second. *Amplitude* measures the magnitude of the waveform; this relates the strength or power of that electrical signal at a point in time. *Phase* refers to the degree to which two particular signals are mathematically aligned (congruent or harmonious) or misaligned (different). A waveform at its peak (highest point) can be assigned a value of 1.0 and at its nadir (lowest point) of -1.0. If the waveform consists purely of a single frequency, it is known as a sine wave. If it truly consists of only a single frequency, it remains of constant amplitude. Any change in amplitude brings in other frequencies until the signal settles down again.

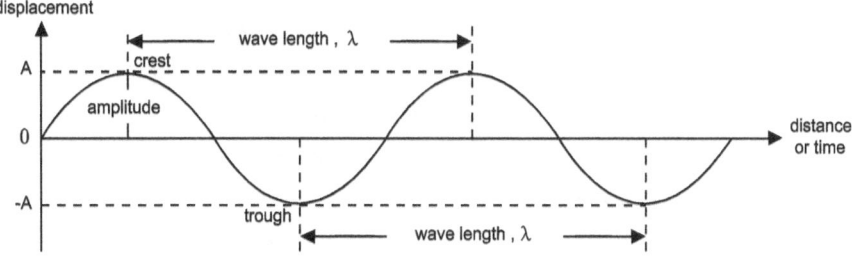

Signals from two sites are said to be *in phase* when their amplitudes reach peak (+1) and nadir (-1) simultaneously. They are *out of phase* when one signal approaches +1 and the other approaches -1 simultaneously. (When two signals are perfectly in phase, they are said to be *synchronous*.)

Thus any two waveforms—brainwave electrical impulses—may be measured and compared in terms of their phase relationship—that is, the extent to which they are congruent (similar) or disparate (different). Congruence or similarity is known as *synchronous* activity. Disparate or difference in phase is known as *asynchronous* activity. Our brains need and function with both synchronous and asynchronous rhythms.

Asynchronous activity allows for independence of nerve function, promoting and establishing flexibility. As an analogy, it allows the left and right hand to play different notes or different rhythms. Asynchronous brain activity fosters independent and discrete functions, the multitasking of life, and the abilities to operate with varying timing, which are vital for the operation of and discernment between different activities and events. Asynchronous activity allows us to respond to changing conditions (including metabolic survival needs), threat or danger, to learn new information and to problem solve. Asynchronous activity forms the essence of flexibility, the capacity and habit of shifting to mobilize the states and resources conducive to ever changing situations and demands.

Synchronous activity allows for harmony, the coalescence of similar functions and teamwork—strength in numbers and synergy. Synchronous activity allows the brain to "rest" and operate in a relaxed and composed manner, even in the midst of intense work. It's easy to think of a sports team or orchestra playing together in unison, even as individual members contribute different portions. When you are sleeping or digesting well, or when you are focused and absorbed in an activity without a noticeable stress reaction, you are operating with a predominance of synchronous activity in your brain and nervous system.

Our nervous systems operate with complementary functions of fight-or-flight and relaxation. However, the interplay of asynchronous and synchronous activity is more complicated. Even in stress responses, our nerves may be recruited to synchronous response in a state of emergency. In such situations, we are "harmonious," but not relaxed or peaceful. Many cases of physical injury result in too much neurological synchrony, such as when a stroke victim loses the perceptual and motor abilities to distinguish and control fine body sensations. Cognitive impairment debilitates, by degrees, the capacity to discern essential organizing principles that allow for concept formation and stability, new learning, and effective generalization to new experiences. Emotional impairment and trauma tend to recruit narrow nervous system responses that keep people stuck in past events and automatic overly synchronous responses.

Conversely, when the brain is very disorganized (e.g., from prolonged stress, injury, illness, or genetic/developmental irregularities), too much *disorganized* asynchronous activity may prevail, resulting in pronounced states of dysfunction and distress. Flexibility develops from organized asynchronous activity, interspersed with synchronous activity that fosters and supports neurological stability, self-regulation, and routine self-soothing.

The key concept is that optimal and adaptive brain functioning depends upon the contributions and checks and balances of asynchronous and synchronous activity. When our brains are balanced and adaptive electrically, we can respond with both flexibility and harmony.

HARNESSING OSCILLATION FOR CONTROL

Since there are natural variations and fluctuations in the oscillating rhythms within us (and around us), the objective is not to invoke or force a particular rhythm. Instead the idea is to recognize and facilitate the adaptive transitions between and among the naturally occurring oscillations that comprise our states and their changes.

When the brain is functioning well, it automatically shifts from one oscillating rhythm to another in response to internal and external cues and conditions. For instance, when it's time for sleep, the brain needs to transition into sleep mode—typically downshifting to slower EEG rhythms that are compatible with sleep states.

When conditions call for concentration and problem-solving, the brain utilizes a predominance of faster wave activity for these tasks. In the event (or perception) of emergency or danger, the brain and nervous system summon a heightened arousal or vigilance, typically familiar as fight-or-flight mode.

From a biophysical perspective, the interplay and confluence of asynchronous and synchronous EEG activity comprise the self-regulation of the brain and nervous system. Well-regulated brains interchange and arrange the many levels of EEG activity in an organized and complementary fashion, allowing for flexible and variable response patterns to changing conditions. When the brain is "dysregulated," many types of symptoms, distress, and illness can ensue.

How can you harness this oscillation principle to help you gain more control?

You can develop better control by improving your flexibility and harmony (asynchronous and synchronous activity) through an understanding of activities that support these brain capacities and through deliberate and systematic exercises to augment and fine-tune them.

IMPROVING YOUR FLEXIBILITY AND HARMONY

We have many ways we can improve our flexibility and harmony, thereby increasing our health, contentment, and productivity. Nature assists this process in that physical activities and "three-dimensional" behavior (acting in the world) promote neurological stability and change, modifying inner activity through "mental" exercises that modify, in turn, the flexibility and harmony within the brain and nervous system.

ASYNCHRONOUS TRAINING

You can improve your brain's flexibility through invoking and befriending the challenge process (described extensively in my book,

Living Intact: Challenge and Choice in Tough Times), which I will summarize here.

Challenge is a phenomenon that occurs at the infinitesimal levels of our cells and at the colossal levels of the larger environment and universe. Regulating our moods or being able to get a better night's sleep are significant conquests at a personal level. Challenges may be physical (such as getting through the day when tired or stressed; attaining a better level of fitness), emotional (such as dealing with difficult people or "tests" of our emotional stamina), logistical (organizing and planning), and cognitive (learning new or difficult material).

Though challenge may sometimes be competitive, its comprehensive value is in the process of adapting the brain and body to better levels of accommodation and flexibility. When you strive to meet challenges, you are engaging your brain's use of asynchronous activity to become more flexible and better able to shift state and set of resources to meet the challenge.

The intensity, strain, and focus that come with physical or cognitive exercises develop flexibility, as well as skills and confidence. You may intuitively or experientially know that such endeavors produce these attributes. Add to this the knowledge that our brain responds to challenges by practicing and improving its asynchronous functions.

Dealing with stress, conflict, and insufficient reward are not only endemic to life—they are the training grounds for improving asynchronous flexibility to better adapt to varied and evolving demands.

The other side of the coin involving brain balance is the continuity and regulation of synchronous activity. Our brains need rest, simultaneity, predictability, recovery, and reward in order to sustain replenishment, interest, motivation, self-protection, and inner harmony.

SYNCHRONOUS TRAINING

Synchronous activity contributes to harmony. These naturally occurring life forces express themselves externally through "being on the same page" as others and internally by experiences of self-regulation, peacefulness, relaxation, and the flow of reward that the brain experiences. Though synchronous activity (as well as asynchronous activity) may occur during exertion, the nature of synchrony is composure, a fitting together of compatibles.

We accept the necessity of relaxation, the ability to calm ourselves, and the importance of schedules and health-inducing habits (often easier said than done routinely). By understanding the concept of synchrony and how it underpins your brain's ability to regulate and control what's important, we can more purposefully direct our energies to providing the balance our brain needs to function more optimally.

When you sleep and when you relax (assuming your brain is reasonably self-regulated and not "disrupted" by seizures, panic, extended overreactions, etc.), your brain is clocking along with synchronous rhythms. These are more or less "happy" and restorative brainwaves.

For most people who are so accustomed, a drink of alcohol or moderate exercise will also induce synchronous rhythms. For some people, positive thoughts, looking forward to events, or engaging in familiar routines may also shift the brain into an abundance of synchronous activity.

It surprises some to know that *love* is a major contributor to synchronous, beneficial brain activity. Love, affection, compassion, and empathy do more than feel good; these experiences are vital for healthy and restorative brain function. The wonderful news is that we can create and repeat these brain harmonizing experiences from our own will and intention in the very circumstances in which we find ourselves. (Of course there are challenges for everybody—this incorporates the asynchronous, flexibility component.)

Engaging volitionally in activities, experiences, thoughts, and feelings that promote synchrony in your brain are effective and strategic ways to improve your health, satisfaction, and productivity. A varied mix of work, relationship, self-care, and recreational activities naturally provide the brain with practice in asynchronous and synchronous neural activity to foster flexibility and harmony. In addition, just as a physical fitness or rehab regimen can target and augment specific body fitness, there is a recognized way to do this for the brain.

SPECIFICALLY TRAINING ASYNCHRONOUS AND SYNCHRONOUS BRAIN ACTIVITY

A proven viable way to directly train the organization and efficiency of brain activity through electronically mediated exercises is a technique that has been around for decades, and is becoming progressively more refined: EEG neurofeedback (also called EEG biofeedback or simply neurofeedback or biofeedback). The procedure directly trains the brainwaves through the use of computers and specific, carefully calibrated software. The program is based on electrical brain activity measured by an electroencephalogram (EEG).

Neurofeedback permits the brain to function more efficiently and proficiently by taking advantage of the brain's *plasticity*, or ability to adapt and utilize different aspects of itself whenever such flexibility is advantageous. During neurofeedback training, you (and the practitioner) observe your brain in action from moment to moment. You can see this information on a computer screen and simultaneously reward your brain for changing its activity to more appropriate patterns. This gradual learning process affects and conditions any measurable aspect of brain function.

Neurofeedback is training in self-regulation, which is a necessary part of good brain function. Self-regulation training makes the brain and central nervous system function more capably.

Neurofeedback works by giving the brain a chance to see itself in action, the same process by which the brain learns a motor skill. But in the neurofeedback process, instead of the brain seeing itself shooting baskets, it observes its own EEG. This simple process of self-observation allows it to improve shooting skills (in one example) as well as its own self-regulatory capacity (in the other). At the top level, neurofeedback involves monitoring brainwaves and converting these electrical signals from the scalp into digital information that in turn governs various visual, auditory, and/or tactile feedback pathways. The brain picks up on that information and acts upon it in its own best interests.

To do this, a clinician attaches electrode sensors to the scalp. Nothing goes into the head via these wires—neither electric current nor information. The sensors simply monitor and conduct the signal from the head and brain to an amplifier, and from there to one or more computers.

The computer equipment digitally transforms your brain signals into audiovisual information, usually presented in the form of a variety of engaging entertainment. While your brain is being trained, you watch the "movie" or "play" the game for about thirty minutes at a time, and you influence the feedback by controlling it with your brainwaves! The marvel of electronics makes this possible, but the key to its efficacy lies in the technology of filtering your brainwaves, and in the science of selecting the range of signals your brain should alter in order for you to feel and function better.

Of the many ways in which we learn and use new information or organize and modify our habits, neurofeedback involves very efficient learning at deep levels of brain neural activity—the levels at which asynchronous and synchronous activity originate.

The distinguishing features of neurofeedback:

- Learning is initiated at a neurological level by training brain behavior, to which people may not feel strongly connected, and for which they may not feel particular responsibility. But when brain behavior is normalized, outward behavior follows. Eventually, life becomes more manageable, often with little additional conscious effort.

- You are a witness to your own brain in action. You watch it meander from success to struggle and back again. The neurofeedback process teaches you about your visible behavior while your brain is simultaneously learning about itself in a unique and replicable way.

- Learning accelerates and behavior modifies rapidly and efficiently (evoking thousands of reinforcements per session).

- Brain abilities develop that translate to other situations in life. This is because these abilities are fundamental, allowing your brain to remain calm, organized, and focused, whereas otherwise it might escalate into too much excitability or lapse into disorganization.

THE MECHANICS AND MATHEMATICS OF ASYNCHRONOUS AND SYNCHRONOUS BRAIN ACTIVITY

Discussing brain activity measurement earlier, I referred to the concepts of *frequency*, *amplitude*, and *phase relationships*. Let's recall these terms in order to explain how we can train the brain for better asynchrony and synchrony, thus developing better flexibility and harmony.

When an electrode is placed on the scalp, it samples the signal coming from that area (site) and displays the information as a cycle ranging from a peak of +A to -A. The height A of the wave is measured in *microvolts* (millionths of a volt) and is displayed in an undulating line a certain number of times per second (frequency). For example, a brainwave pattern of 12 Hz at 75 microvolts means there are twelve up-and-down complete cycles each second. Each cycle includes a peak of +A and a nadir of -A, where A refers to its particular amplitude. The point at which the waveform crosses from plus to minus in each cycle can be assigned the phase value of zero. Phase values for each waveform vary continuously and smoothly until the wave undergoes a complete cycle and then repeats.

In training the brain for better performance and flexibility, clinicians are able address the modifications of frequency, amplitude, and phase.

TRAINING FREQUENCIES

Our brains operate with multiple frequencies, ranging from the EEG range (from 0.5 Hz upward) down through the *infralow frequency* (ILF) range (below 0.1 Hz). We can train the ranges typically associated with muscle and cognitive operations (typically with concentrated activity somewhere within selected bandwidths in the 4-80 Hz range) and with primitive emotional and developmental functions (we often train below 0.01 Hz). Our brains transmit electrical impulses constantly among nerve cells along many pathways that utilize different frequencies simultaneously. When we intervene to "invite" and influence the brain to alter even a few of these circuits at a given frequency range, we powerfully affect a variety of neural networks in the brain.

By "rewarding" certain frequencies and "inhibiting" others, we can train the brain to become comfortable using a preponderance of certain time signatures that facilitate better operations in certain circumstances and with certain activities. We refer to this process as enabling *state management*. For example, slower brainwave activity (which we have all the time) is better suited to relaxation and sleep, whereas faster frequencies are needed for cognitive problem-solving, physical activities, and emergency response. Brain training results in better abilities to "shift" into the state most appropriate for and conducive to the task at hand.

TRAINING AMPLITUDES

Besides influencing the brain's adaptation to more functional state management frequencies, we can train *amplitude*—that is, influencing the strength and power of brain activity associated with particular functions, such as vigor, focus, relaxation, creativity, etc. Increasingly though, we find that training *phase relationships* among neurons yields tremendous results in promoting the blend of asynchronous and synchronous activity.

TRAINING PHASE RHYTHMS

Phase training involves training the phase relationship between two sites in order to promote *phase differences*. This procedure trains the brain's ability to meet challenges, become more flexible, and problem solve automatically without conscious reasoning. This is because the timing relationship between different brain sites is the most critical variable when it comes to the brain's internal communication in connection with state management.

Here's how it works: Electrodes are placed at two scalp sites during each training period, and the rewards (moments when the movie effects or video game progress) are set to occur when the *two sites show phase differences in activity*. I will explain this mathematically first then relate it to improvements in brain activity and daily life.

Signals from two sites are said to be *in phase* when their amplitudes reach peak (+1) and nadir (-1) simultaneously. They are *out of phase* when one signal approaches +1 and the other approaches -1 simultaneously. (When two signals are perfectly in phase, they are said to be *synchronous.*) As you train by playing the video game, your brain is intermittently rewarded for "figuring out" how to make the frequency cycles from each site occur at slightly different times. ("You" think you are piloting a spaceship on the screen, while your brain is in the control room, working furiously to figure out the timing codes to keep things moving.) In phase-based training, the reward is not based on the amplitude, but rather on the timing differences between when each of the two signals reaches that amplitude. Mathematically, the rewards occur when the differences become greater (i.e., move away from zero toward an absolute value of one, either positive or negative).

You can think of this as similar to teaching instrumentalists in an orchestra to play different notes at the same time (or teaching your hands to play different notes on the piano at staggered time intervals). The effects of this kind of flexibility are astounding and infinite. When you can master playing different notes in varying combinations of time synchrony, you are becoming a master, perhaps eventually a virtuoso.

Taking the musical analogy a step further, phase training is like teaching the brain to sing in harmony, in choral rounds, and in synchrony, as needed. Phase training tunes and trains your brain modules to coordinate among themselves and to communicate with the outside world like a practiced and well-timed group of musicians. Most of us are familiar with singing in staggered choral rounds; remember the song, "Row, Row, Row Your Boat"? When two groups sing it together, they are in phase, and the timing code looks like this:

GROUP 1

Row, row, row your boat	Gently down the stream	Merrily, merrily, merrily, merrily,	Life is but a dream.

GROUP 2

Row, row, row your boat	Gently down the stream	Merrily, merrily, merrily, merrily,	Life is but a dream.

However, when they sing in choral rounds, they are out of phase, and it looks like this:

GROUP 1

Row, row, row your boat	Gently down the stream	Merrily, merrily, merrily, merrily,	Life is but a dream.

GROUP 2

Merrily, merrily, merrily, merrily,	Life is but a dream.	Row, row, row your boat	Gently down the stream

Singing in rounds, and transitioning back to unison, requires careful attention, as well as the ability to focus narrowly and then expand that focus to incorporate the context and its sequence and timing. In order to do this properly, you must be able to shift as necessary. This is a complex task, yet most elementary school students are able to do it (provided that their brains are functioning well). When your brain can shift time codes and integrate and adapt different timing mechanisms, you can pay attention, screen out distractions, maintain continuity, sift and shift to accommodate salient details, and follow a task through to its conclusion.

If improving your brain flexibility and harmony something you want to be able to do better and more consistently, neurofeedback— and phase training in particular—will help you far along that path. When your brain learns to differentiate its timing mechanisms (which is what phase training conditions it to do), you progressively achieve the following:

- Freedom from symptoms;
- Improved performance and efficiency;
- Better, quicker accessibility to appropriate responses;
- Faster recovery from fatigue and stress;
- More endurance;
- Greatly enhanced flexibility;
- Less vulnerability to overreactions;
- Better self-regulation and self-control;
- Enhanced creativity;
- Better concentration;
- Improved perception and coordination;
- Better sensitivity to people;
- Reduced carelessness;
- Less defensiveness, hypervigilance, or fight/flight mode;
- Increased empathy, compassion, contentment;

- Reduced tendency to become overwhelmed or absorbed by pain; and

- Improved ability to filter distractions, focus sharply, and multitask.

For the novice, EEG neurofeedback should be administered and guided by an experienced professional. After establishing a basic regimen that elicits positive results (typically enduring), most laypeople can learn to self-administer neurofeedback (hopefully with periodic check-in supervision with a professional), using appropriate and recommended equipment.

BOTTOM LINE RESULTS

Anyone who has read this far probably has great interest, patience, and an admirable tolerance for details. Though the electrophysiological principles are fascinating to me, I realize that for most others, they are complicated, boring, and esoteric. Even as I explain a very simplified version of these principles, I'm reminded of sitting in excruciating math classes (some of which I taught in graduate school), laboring through theorems and proofs, when what was really desired was to get to the correct answer. The methodology and hope were and are that the right science, closely monitored, evaluated, and adjusted, will lead to better quality of lives for the majority.

As stated at the beginning, the interplay between harmony (compatible synchronous activity) and opposition (contrasting challenge and asynchronous activity) is fundamental to the order of the universe, to nature, science, and life. The flexibility that develops through interspersing these complements spawns survival and productivity.

To the extent that we can improve and maintain flexibility and harmony, we are in line with the realities that govern the operations of our universe and our brains.

OSCILLATION IN PRACTICE

In addition to understanding, physiologically sensing, and training your own patterns of oscillation, you can become aware of how underlying oscillations affect behaviors and attitudes, the general ambience of groups and relationships, and the interactions you have with others. When you are "in sync" with someone else (or perhaps a team), you can assume that the oscillation patterns between and among you are *resonating*—that is, establishing patterns of harmony and/or complementary oscillations that feel good and work well. As you become more cognizant of your own rhythms and better able to change or control them (shift internal state), you will more easily and fluidly adapt and "get on the same wavelength" as the person with whom you are trying to communicate or relate. Matching your internal state to the situation will occur much more naturally.

You don't need to measure oscillations. With practice in developing your flexibility, harmony, and self-control, you do better at sensing the oscillations around and within you, thus automatically adjusting and fitting the situation with rhythms that will facilitate desired and positive outcomes.

CHAPTER 8

PRESSURE

Contact and Force

The last principle to support efforts to take charge and get ahead is the principle of *pressure*. Pressure is a continuous physical force exerted on or against an object by something in contact with it. Alternately, is the use of persuasion, influence, or intimidation to make someone do something.

We all face pressures in life on a continuing basis. Our internal systems notify us of routine biological needs, like eating and going to the bathroom, needing rest, and sensing pain or discomfort when something is wrong or dangerous.

Pressure arises from the needs and demands of others, as well as from our own responsibilities. Few people are free from financial pressure, and fewer still are unburdened from battles with self-discipline or the unrelenting stimulus of ambitions or unfulfilled goals.

Two aspects of pressure are related to control:

1. Pressure exerted upon you, and
2. Pressure you exert upon the world.

PRESSURE EXERTED UPON YOU

Life is full of demands, responsibilities, costs, deadlines and time constraints, and other impositions that require responses. These "pressures" are comprised of known factors as well as sudden or unanticipated issues. People respond to pressures in different ways. Some people handle stress better than others. An objective in improving your life control is for you to develop ways to cope with pressure that allow you to do the following:

- Sort out reasonable from unreasonable expectations (a.k.a., the doable and not doable).
- Plan your responses and choose effective and productive courses of action.
- Keep your nervous system and emotions under control despite demands, adversity, and conflict.
- Maintain your perspective according to proper contexts in which you respond to pressures.
- Set limits on what others expect or require of you.
- Develop adequate internal recovery from tasks and people that deplete you.

Some people appear to let pressure "roll like water off a duck's back." While it may be true that these folks seem to manage life with more aplomb, you don't really know how they are internalizing and regulating stress. Appearances can be deceiving (and/or defensive or posturing). They may actually be managing well, or they could be hiding and building up internal pressure that deflates health and results in maladaptive habits to cope or let off steam.

Others are more perfectionistic. They react to or interpret demand situations by overresponding, setting exceedingly high standards, favoring details and perfection over deadlines, or behaving in persistently rigid or meticulous ways, rather than being flexible. Such individuals put pressure on themselves, as well as holding others to very high standards. Conscientiousness and accountability notwith-standing, pressure must be *accommodated and managed* so that *effective-ness and control are maintained and regulated.*

In order to take care of ourselves and others and get things done, we must feel and respond to pressure. Think of pressure on a contin-uum as a curvilinear representation of arousal: with little awareness of or response to pressure, internal arousal is low, thus favoring a re-laxation response with lower motivation. As pressure is perceived and arousal heightens, there is more energy and imperative to act in order to meet the demand and relieve the pressure. At the farther end of the curve, increased pressure increases overarousal and anxiety and tends to diminish motivation and favor avoidance in the service of lowering stress and preserving energy and equanimity. Thus pressure exerted upon you can have a motivating and energizing effect as long as it is not overwhelming, either in perception or actuality.

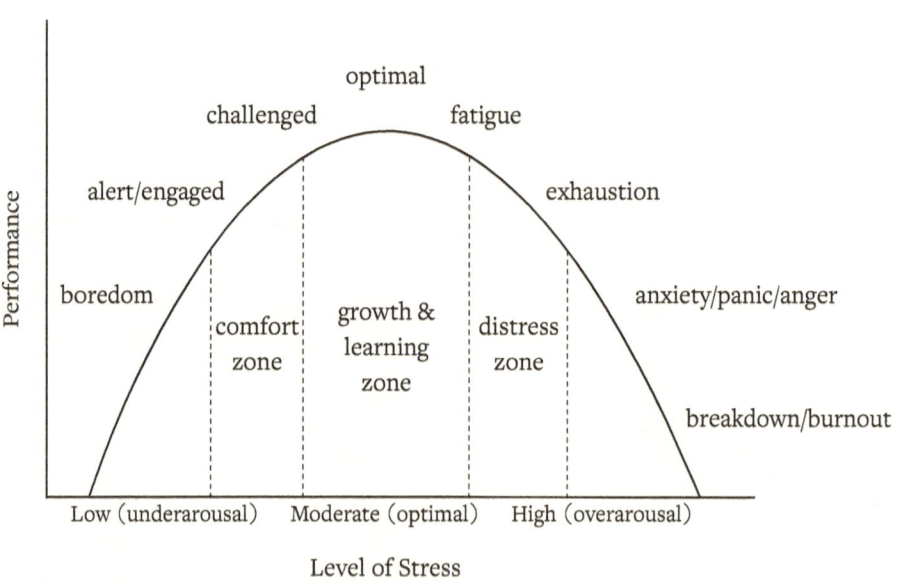

DETERMINE REASONABLE EXPECTATIONS

In the hustle and bustle of daily life, you likely face many demands, responsibilities, and "have to's." Juggling work, family, errands, self-care, and the host of things that come up can be overwhelming. Frankly, it's remarkable that many of us do as much as we do—albeit often at a cost of stress, partial accomplishment, and taking on too much.

Planning your responses and commitments and to budget your time, energy, and money is vital. For any given demand, sudden urgency or expense, it may be tempting or doable to accommodate. In the long run however, you need to allot your limited personal and material resources so you don't over commit, overspend, or burn out.

No one can "do it all." Some people have boundless energy or ambition. Others find it hard to say no. Wherever you are on the spectrum of responding to burgeoning or unceasing demands, you can deal with pressure effectively by determining in advance what you can do and what could be the "straw that breaks the camel's back." The following steps may be helpful in determining reasonable expectations for yourself, regardless of the continuing pressures:

a) Keep a calendar, schedule, and/or to-do list. Update it routinely. Seeing this on paper will put into perspective what is doable and what may be excessive. Though you may at times want to stretch to accommodate more, you can at least see what you are taking on with respect to the bigger picture.

b) Separate the impositions from your environment from the demands you place on yourself. You can't be in two places at once, and you can't accede to everyone's requests—obviously. But take the time to sort it out and reason it through.

c) Examine your track record by reviewing your past experiences with responding to demands and pressures. How are you at saying *no* . . . or *later*? How do you feel when you take on lotto much or overexert? How keen is your judgment about budgeting and planning your output and commitments?

EXAMPLE 2

RECOGNIZE THE "PRESSURE COOKER" AND AVOID UNDUE STRESS

You probably know yourself well enough to sense how you deal with pressure and stress. Some people perform better under strict deadlines. Some even use procrastination as a tool or default to get themselves to perform "under the gun" (usually ill-advised). Others mount avoidance or simply shut down.

You want to marshal pressure only to motivate you and work in your favor, not to make you become irritable or come apart. Remember the arousal curve: some degree of arousal is helpful to get going. When arousal becomes excessive, it defeats motivation and efficiency and introduces negative attitudes and physiological effects. (These interactions vary greatly among individuals.)

Reasonably well-regulated individuals may respond positively to external pressures because they enjoy meeting the needs of others by being reliable and/or sacrificing. As long as you can manage stress loads, pressures from the outside world can serve to sharpen you, increase your productivity, and propel you to achieve goals and meet needs.

In the area of finances (as well as self-management and activities), be aware of how much effort you must maintain to meet and pay for the standard of living you set. Bills must be paid, and material things are important and pleasurable. However, know where your money is going, whether your income/assets and expenses are balanced and sustainable, and—importantly—whether your hard work is worth the rewards they earn or command.

EXAMPLE 3

AVOIDING SELF–DEFEATING STANDARDS AND RESPONSIBILITIES

In keeping with the guidelines discussed above, come to terms with the standards you set for yourself, as well as the number of obligations you encumber. Easier said than done of course, as things have a way of piling up. But you have choices in these matters, especially over discretionary ventures and obligations, and the standards you may set for yourself that could be too perfectionistic or depleting.

Is that social event really necessary? How much more detail or review does that paper or presentation require? Do you have to pick up the slack again for a coworker or family member?

Though it's good to serve others and to be habitually conscientious and responsible, allowing perfectionism or wanting to do too much is often not only a habit, but a way of responding to anxieties by overworking or overpromising. Take stock and be honest with yourself. Seek advice, feedback, or mentoring to curtail or refine tendencies you may have to overdo things or strive for overly exact or unattainable standards.

EXAMPLE 4

SETTING LIMITS ON OTHERS

Saying no can be difficult. It can also elicit pushback or negative consequences. Just as the family dog begs at the dinner table until you firmly discourage and train out this behavior, others may encroach, push, ask, wheedle, manipulate, and demand.

Sometimes it's obvious; at other times, you don't even realize the extent or impropriety of the demands until you review your history with certain persons. It's especially difficult to set limits *after* the habit of acquiescing or performing has taken hold. Naturally, the receiving party expects things from you, based upon past experience and your service or capitulation. In the dog example, even one table scrap interspersed with many refusals will revive and encourage continued begging. You have to be firm. Though difficult at first, it gets easier.

In some situations, setting limits may seem to or actually threaten your job or other security. A very sensitive and common example (in the workplace and in personal relationships) is rebuffing sexual overtures or advances. If you don't give in, he may sulk, pout, manipulate, threaten, or end the relationship. Standing your ground has consequences, but you will have to live with yourself and your values.

It's hard to say no or set limits on excessive work demands. In conjunction with cracking the whip on yourself (often at the expense of sleep, relaxation, or family), the exigencies of employer (and customer) demands seem to burgeon exponentially. Societal changes (like a pandemic, social division, inflation), corporate mismanagement, retrenchment, or unreasonableness can compile to place more duties and expectations upon you than you ever had or signed up for. Setting limits can be a diplomatic negotiation that nudges the other party to face reality:

a) When given too much work or too strict a deadline, as you defer, pay lip service to the requesting party's need and own pressure. "I realize you are under deadlines and you have too much work to do, and I'd love to help as much as I can. I'm flattered that you depend upon me, and I don't want to disappoint you. Frankly, I can't undertake or finish what you're asking. I would if I could, but that's simply not realistic now."

b) Negotiate a compromise or delay. "That's an overloading task. Perhaps I could do a part of it (specify) and the other part can be delegated or deferred to another date."

c) At times, you have to set firm limits: "I can't work this weekend. I have other commitments made previously that are important and not cancelable."

PRESSURE YOU EXERT UPON THE WORLD

As you act to meet your needs, acquire goods or services, work with people and serve them, you make impacts upon your surroundings and those with whom you interact. When you give an instruction, place an order, or request that someone perform or help, you are exerting *pressure*.

By expressing or exerting contact or force, you are shaping those around you, though not necessarily manipulating. Pressure simply achieves (or tries to achieve) an effect upon someone or some situation to mobilize a response being sought or expected. Pressure is a stimulus that announces, calls for, or describes a requested response.

Inertia is an energy principle that underscores how a body at rest is likely to remain at rest, whereas a body in motion tends to remain in motion. In other words, inertia describes the resistance of any physical object to a change in its velocity. Thus to make changes, take charge, and move ahead, we need to constantly change inertia by adjusting pressure to overcome resistance and mobilize toward desired results.

Just as we respond to pressures upon us, we must consciously take charge of the way we use pressure outwardly to create favorable bearing upon our environment. The idea of pressure conjures images and negative emotional reactions of being monopolized or forced against one's will. While certainly there are times and situations where pressure will invoke resentment or pushback, exerting pressure in adaptive ways is a normal tactic to influence behavior and communicate the times and conditions for things to happen.

Here are some examples of the intrinsic use of pressure in daily life:

EXAMPLE 1

ACCOUNTABILITY

Necessary activities in daily life require that we keep our word and commitments, follow through on tasks and responsibilities, and "own" our mistakes and involvement when things don't go well. Accountability is the general category that subsumes these attitudes and behaviors. Accountability comprises a set of skills and attitudes that are learned through experience and maturity. The opposite of this would be disownership, dismissal, forgetfulness, or blaming others or external events for one's failure to perform.

When accountability flags or is absent, things tend to break down. Duties and promises are left unfulfilled, resentment grows, and the "tight ship" of functionality and trust gradually drifts.

For many people, holding others accountable is difficult, fraught with anxiety, and tenuous. *What will he think of me if I call him on his lack of follow-through? What if he brings up my mistakes or shortcomings? If I make this a big deal, she may resent me.*

Indeed when people are accustomed to doing things their way (partially, tardily, shoddily, or not at all), they don't want to be held to account. Often their immature resistance surfaces in the form of defensiveness, excuse making, or irritation at "being blamed." Thus it will take fortitude, self-confidence, poise, and lots of practice to communicate *facts* regarding someone's accountability, while taking care to focus on the events and their consequences rather than on negative emotions that may accompany both parties when such issues are raised.

"You said you would be home at the agreed-upon time for dinner. You were over an hour late. That left me and the family waiting hungrily, while the food got cold."

(Not: "Where were you? You always do this and leave us hanging!")

"Last night, you left dirty dishes in the living room. I had to clean up so there wouldn't be bugs and disarray. You have done this multiple times in the past two weeks."

"You agreed to stop drinking during the week. Yet you were drinking every night this week. When you drink, it's difficult to talk with you. You become withdrawn or surly and unlike your normal considerate self."

Holding someone's feet to the fire should not be angry or vindictive. Rather have an honest communication with disclosure about how you depend upon that person and the degree to which they fulfill their promise and integrity. Often you will have to carefully sidestep negative emotional tensions to focus simply on the errant behavior in advance of remaking agreements.

EXAMPLE 2

DEADLINES

In civilized societies, life revolves around deadlines. We are subject not only to the rhythms of nature, but to the pressures imposed by time limits. Bills, papers, and projects are due; people depend upon you as you depend upon them; even goals you set for yourself are guided and governed by expected times of performance or accomplishment. Just as you feel the pressure of meeting deadlines, you can exert pressure upon others by holding them to and/or reminding them about accountability in getting things done on time.

A myriad of intervening factors may delay or warrant the adjustment of originally set timelines. Nonetheless, the need to get things done on an expected schedule affects the people around you and the results you depend upon. When the power goes off or there is a natural disaster, we all desperately wonder when normalcy will be restored. In such cases, even though we're dependent, we cannot force deadlines. We have to wait and accommodate adjustments. We can assume more control by exerting pressure carefully on others whose performance is expected and often promised. If a construction or engineering project is delayed, it causes frustration and increases costs. When your family member fails to follow through and deliver on a task or showing up for a scheduled event, it introduces disruption, delay, and resentment.

EXAMPLE 3

STANDARDS

Along with deadlines, holding others accountable for reasonable and specified standards in what they do is important. You needn't be a micromanager or set overly high criteria. But part of developing and maintaining trusting and dependable relationships involves assurance that others will fulfill their obligations to reasonable degrees of thoroughness and competency.

Whether washing the dishes, grading student performances, or performing employee appraisals, holding people accountable to known standards allows normal pressure to elicit expected performance.

Practice, tact, and the development of good skills are needed to foster learning, encouragement, and motivation—still you need to use the pressure of adherence to standards wisely to ensure that people will be your allies and reflect well on your tutelage and expectations. You can model accountability by setting, meeting, and explaining your personal standards—not omitting your shortcomings, failures to meet your own expectations, or the efforts you exert to perform at reasonable levels and not disappoint others.

Again bear in mind, and in actions, the importance of blending compromise, forgiveness, adjustments, diplomacy, and adherence to agreed-upon values and principles in getting things done and keeping your word. Admitting mistakes, accepting responsibility, and remaking agreements are all parts of aspiring to and achieving satisfactory standards of performance and living.

EXAMPLE 4

FEEDBACK

Giving feedback is an important way of communicating observations, evaluation, and satisfaction with others' performances. Though people don't always request feedback (and may not be receptive to it), providing information about how their actions affect you or measure up is a vital part of staying connected, setting and reviewing expectations, and providing guidance so that others can know and adjust how they relate to you.

In some roles—parenting, teaching, supervising, coaching—feedback is an integral part of the job. By dint of your authority in a particular relationship, feedback exerts some pressure to adjust and conform to your standards.

In peer and intimate relationships, feedback is also a valuable part of building trust, satisfaction, and assurance that you or someone else is doing things well and correctly. It is important to be sensitive and tactful in offering feedback, since your objective should be to constructively recommend and shape the behavior of the recipient. Naturally some individuals are overly sensitive to criticism, have fragile self-esteem, or simply put themselves ahead of others consistently. And even the most sensitive of managers will judge or inadvertently hurt the feelings of someone else. Be sure to integrate and be aware of the role and value that your feedback plays in exerting pressure necessary for others to change and meet or approach your standards.

EXAMPLE 5

STATING NEEDS EXPECTATIONS

All too often, we make mistakes that impair communications or breed resentment in dealing with others. Two common mistakes are: 1) thinking the other person knows what we want or expect, when we have not adequately said so, and/or 2) blaming the other person for failing to meet our expectation or needs.

So you must develop the well-honed habit of clearly letting others know what you want from them and your reason for expecting (or wishing) they would accede. Recognize that communicating your needs and expectations is no assurance that the other party will agree or follow through; but without a clear communication and understanding, you're less likely to get your desired result.

When the other person doesn't comply or follow through, frustration can often lead to critical blaming. This is unproductive and very different from simply reviewing and stating what you wanted and what the other person did or didn't do.

"Bill, I was expecting my car to be ready this afternoon, based upon what we agreed when I brought it in. If that was not realistic, you should have informed me earlier. Now my commitments have been delayed, and my schedule is thrown off."

"Roberta, when you are frustrated or dissatisfied with me or something I did, I'd like you to talk to me calmly (no yelling), and state simply and clearly the facts about what I did or didn't do that made you disappointed or upset. That way, I can more calmly explain and make adjustments to suit you. Thanks."

PRESSURE MAKES US STRONGER

The principles of exercising to improve fitness illustrate the way pressure works to help us. In developing physical fitness, we subject our bodies to exercise that builds strength, endurance, flexibility, and resilience. This necessarily subjects us to pressure against which our bodies respond and rebound. As long as the pressure is measured, gradual, and not overwhelming, pressure can act as our ally.

Just as we experience the effects and consequences of pressure upon ourselves, we need to communicate the consequences of others' actions upon themselves and us. The communication of accountability, consequences, and cause-and-effect is a natural and concerted use of the principle of pressure.

Being cognizant of how we exert pressure on those around us helps us take charge of situations more effectively and direct and negotiate outcomes more to our aims and satisfaction. Remember too that, although the careful and judicious use of pressure will give you more power and control, your influence and satisfaction will ultimately be enhanced by the constant and conscious integration of sensitivity, forgiveness, and compassion directed toward those affected by your thoughts, feelings, and actions.

CHAPTER 9

SIGNIFICANCE, RELEVANCE, USEFULNESS

A Meta View of Implementation

In the preceding chapters, I have introduced and explained seven Life Control principles that help people take charge and get ahead. Congratulations on wading through some complex material and assimilating concepts endemic to the natural forces that govern the outcomes of human behaviors.

The Life Control principles are natural dynamics that—like gravity, fire, and other natural forces—operate within their particular dynamics regardless of what we know or how we harness them. By understanding how they operate, we can assume better control to make them work *for us* and toward the goals and outcomes we desire and pursue.

While theory and rules are important and necessary, practicality dictates that helpful information and techniques should also conform to characteristics that make them directly related to and productive for desired outcomes. Thus the true value of Life Control principles depends upon their adaptation and implementation with *significance, relevance, and usefulness.*

SIGNIFICANCE

Significance is a term conveying that something is meaningful or note-worthy. Something significant catches your attention or has, or could have, an effect on you. Significance stands out and implies prominence or a relationship between factors, variables, or events.

In science, *statistical significance* is determined by mathematical formulas that correlate the relationships among variables and the probabilities that those relationships observed were an actual correlation or cause-and-effect linkage, rather than by chance. Typically, statistical significance is calculated with probability measures. For example, an outcome with a $p<.001$ means that there is less than one out of a thousand chances that the observed outcome was due to chance, rather than a direct relationship between two variables. Another way of describing statistical significance is that of *confidence*—that is, we can be confident that 999 times out of 1,000, a hypothesized relationship exists that resulted in the observed outcome of interest.

Leaving mathematical calculations to the experts, we observe significance all around us. We may rely on professionals to inform us of how meaningful they are. Nevertheless, significance alone does not indicate how or the extent to which factors and occurrences may apply to us individually. Weather events, catastrophes, political changes, medical discoveries, and even traffic events can all be significant—but they may not be important or applicable to me or to you, depending upon individual circumstances.

For that determination, we need to include *relevance*.

RELEVANCE

Relevance is a state or quality of being closely connected, important, or appropriate to a matter at hand. All kinds of things (facts, happenings, principles, etc.) are significant in their own right, but may not be relevant to your needs, situation, or anything concerning you. A weather event or natural disaster thousands of miles away carries great significance for those who live there, but is likely not immediately relevant for you. Side effects for medications you are not taking are significant, but not for you. Carcinogenic substances are certainly important and significant, but only if you were exposed to them. There are significant pregnancy risks; but if you are male, these are not relevant to your own body. The list could go on and on.

Conversely, events and information may be relevant to you, but not of particular significance. For example, the price of homes in your area or the costs of borrowing are relevant, but they may not be significant unless there are recent changes and you are in the market to buy, sell, or borrow.

The level of fuel in your car or how much food you have in your refrigerator are relevant to you of course. But unless you are running low, this information might not be of timely significance. When food and gas prices rise, that becomes significant, relevant, and useful information for most of us.

USEFULNESS

Information and feedback that is significant and/or relevant can guide you in employing the Life Control principles. In order to be practical, however, the information must be *useful*. That is, it must be translated and implemented into your activities and repertoire to help you along toward your goals.

For example, traffic reports of problems are relevant if you are heading out in the direction of the delay. The usefulness comes into play if you hear the reports in time to make a change in your driving, and if you have reasonable alternate routes at your disposal. The duration and context components of your decision will be guided by your available road options.

If you try to alter your diet, food values and choices are certainly significant and relevant. But will these data be useful in aiding your choices and behavior change? My example of hurrying myself away from the family and kitchen areas of my house after dinner, and to brush my teeth and enter the bedroom, proved instrumental in allowing me to avoid dessert without stress or cravings. This little trick—as it becomes a habit—is very useful (as noted in the Probability chapter). Avoiding overeating at night (even if the particular choice of food might not be that significant) renders the probability that I'll not eat more if I leave the family room/kitchen areas a useful adjunct in concert with the other principles to help eat more wisely.

Another example of usefulness (and relevance) is the important concept (explained in the Context chapter) of determining whether an individual's behavior is *in character* or *out of character* regarding what you know about that person. Factoring in knowledge of someone's previous behavior patterns gives you an edge in choosing your most-effective interpretation and response to a particular behavior or event.

The principles of frequency, duration, and others are always dynamically operational as they influence behaviors. However, the usefulness of particular principles depends upon the situations and objectives. Practicing or studying more or on different schedules for a test or performance behooves you to understand and manipulate frequency, duration, and intensity—but are specific to your challenges. If you don't have tests or performances imminent, then manipulating the principles is not relevant or useful for you toward those specific outcomes.

EVALUATING AND USING THE PRINCIPLES

For different behavior change and results, one or more of the Life Control principles may be more salient in the applications suitable for your goals and objectives. In general the principles of probability and context will subsume, encompass, and integrate your application of the other principles. To achieve desired outcomes, you are essentially attempting to change the probabilities in your favor within the contexts available and appropriate for your particular circumstances and needs.

The Life Control principles are designed to help you clarify and implement the naturally occurring forces that influence and shape behaviors, including perceptions, feelings, choices, motivation, and perseverance. By understanding, recognizing, and deliberately identifying the principles that govern outcomes, you are determining how to alter probabilities favorably and how to evaluate the consequences and objective effectiveness of what you and others do.

CONTROL IS KEY

The underlying premise throughout this book is that assuming better control is key to managing outcomes more successfully in order to reach goals and objectives. Control is vital for managing yourself and for determining the outcomes you want. To be in control is to manage issues, events, actions, and plans efficiently and successfully while progressing toward your desired results.

As stated earlier, the difference between success and failure, progress or stagnation, influence or ineffectiveness, often boils down to the issue of being in control. There will always be limits to what any of us as individuals can control, but exercising control over oneself and one's environment can be improved with measurable results by just about anyone who takes stock of and practices the management principles available to us in the natural world. Control is not a static entity. Control is dynamic and constantly changing in response to a flow of conditions. Rather than thinking of control as exerting mastery or establishing authority, consider it more realistically as the vibrant interaction with natural forces and the flexibility to reestablish balance and functionality in accord with varying conditions—as the shifting of expectations and life experiences change us and our values and priorities.

My hope and intention is that the principles of Life Control will enable you to achieve more of what you want and enjoy greater satisfaction over your efforts and competence. As you face challenges to take charge and move ahead, review how the seven principles interact with how you behave, and the effects of your interactions with the forces that operate upon you.

Desires and efforts to take charge and get ahead are varied, just as individuals differ in what's important at any given time. Life Control principles will aid you in improving *self-control*, which is often the key to controlling your effectiveness in the world around you. There are limits to how much we can control about others and the circumstances with which we must contend. We can, however, improve much of what you can influence with the tools and circumstances you have.

For many people, exerting better control over mind and body presents major challenges. For others, learning to live more peacefully and with better adjustment to constraining conditions become the necessary and imminent challenges.

You need not scrutinize or implement each and all of the seven principles in every endeavor. Simply recognizing how they work and learning to manipulate some of them to your advantage where possible will improve things for you immensely.

I have tried to boil down scientific principles into accessible language and real life examples. In a follow-up book, I hope to detail and apply more practical ways you can make the Life Control principles work for you. For now, use what you can from this material and move forward with increasing knowledge and success.

I would really like to hear from you.

Mark Steinberg
mark@marksteinberg.com

Want to find out how much you've learned?
Take the **Life Control Test**:
https://marksteinberg.com/life_control_test.do

Dr. Steinberg offers individual services,
as well as seminars and trainings.

For more information, call (408) 356-1002
and visit **www.marksteinberg.com**.

ABOUT THE AUTHOR

Dr. Mark Steinberg is a licensed psychologist with expertise in clinical, educational, and neuropsychology. Throughout a practice spanning four decades, Dr. Steinberg has administered more than 100,000 evaluation and treatment procedures, treating children, adolescents, and adults. He offers a range of services dealing with attention and mood disorders, behavior problems, family and communication issues, developmental disabilities, educational and learning problems, parenting challenges, habit change, addictions, and neurological disorders (including headaches, seizures, and sleep disorders).

By blending the latest technological advances with traditional and scientific methods, Dr. Steinberg improves functioning and eliminates problems that have often persisted for years. He is well-known for his pioneering work with EEG neurofeedback and Voice Technology treatment that eliminates negative emotions in minutes.

Widely consulted as a medical expert, and the winner of local and statewide awards, Dr. Steinberg has made many appearances on local and national television, offering psychological expertise on topics pertaining to health, behavior, and how to live a more satisfying and productive life. His other books include: *Reality Reports: Essays on Mental, Emotional, Spiritual, and Social Issues in the Twenty-First Century; When God Takes Away: Living with Loss and Surrender; Confessions of a Maverick Mind: A Psychologist Shares Stories and Adventures, Essays and Articles, and Poems and Songs; Staying Madly in Love with Your Spouse: Guide to a Happier Marriage;* and *Living Intact: Challenge and Choice in Tough Times.* He coauthored *ADD: The 20-Hour Solution* with Siegfried Othmer, PhD.